Data Center Networking
Complete Self-Assessment Guide

C000311766

The guidance in this Self-Assessment is base~~d~~
Networking best practices and standards in ~~b~~
architecture, design and quality management. Ine guidance is also based
on the professional judgment of the individual collaborators listed in the
Acknowledgments.

Notice of rights

Trademarks

Table of Contents

About The Art of Service

The Art of Service, Business Process Architects since 2000, is dedicated to helping stakeholders achieve excellence.

Defining, designing, creating, and implementing a process to solve a stakeholders challenge or meet an objective is the most valuable role… In EVERY group, company, organization and department.

Unless you're talking a one-time, single-use project, there should be a process. Whether that process is managed and implemented by humans, AI, or a combination of the two, it needs to be designed by someone with a complex enough perspective to ask the right questions.

Someone capable of asking the right questions and step back and say, 'What are we really trying to accomplish here? And is there a different way to look at it?'

With The Art of Service's Standard Requirements Self-Assessments, we empower people who can do just that — whether their title is marketer, entrepreneur, manager, salesperson, consultant, Business Process Manager, executive assistant, IT Manager, CIO etc... —they are the people who rule the future. They are people who watch the process as it happens, and ask the right questions to make the process work better.

Contact us when you need any support with this Self-Assessment and any help with templates, blue-prints and examples of standard documents you might need:

http://theartofservice.com
service@theartofservice.com

Acknowledgments

This checklist was developed under the auspices of The Art of Service, chaired by Gerardus Blokdyk.

Representatives from several client companies participated in the preparation of this Self-Assessment.

In addition, we are thankful for the design and printing services provided.

Included Resources - how to access

Included with your purchase of the book is the Data Center Networking Self-Assessment Spreadsheet Dashboard which contains all questions and Self-Assessment areas and auto-generates insights, graphs, and project RACI planning - all with examples to get you started right away.

How? Simply send an email to
access@theartofservice.com
with this books' title in the subject to get the Data Center Networking Self Assessment Tool right away.

You will receive the following contents with New and Updated specific criteria:

• The latest quick edition of the book in PDF

• The latest complete edition of the book in PDF, which criteria correspond to the criteria in...

• The Self-Assessment Excel Dashboard, and...

• Example pre-filled Self-Assessment Excel Dashboard to get familiar with results generation

• In-depth specific Checklists covering the topic

• Project management checklists and templates to assist with implementation

INCLUDES LIFETIME SELF ASSESSMENT UPDATES

Every self assessment comes with Lifetime Updates and Lifetime Free Updated Books. Lifetime Updates is an industry-first feature which allows you to receive verified self assessment updates, ensuring you always have the most accurate information at your fingertips.

Get it now- you will be glad you did - do it now, before you forget.

Send an email to **access@theartofservice.com** with this books' title in the subject to get the Data Center Networking Self Assessment Tool right away.

Your feedback is invaluable to us

If you recently bought this book, we would love to hear from you! You can do this by writing a review on amazon (or the online store where you purchased this book) about your last purchase! As part of our continual service improvement process, we love to hear real client experiences and feedback.

How does it work?
To post a review on Amazon, just log in to your account and click on the Create Your Own Review button (under Customer Reviews) of the relevant product page. You can find examples of product reviews in Amazon. If you purchased from another online store, simply follow their procedures.

What happens when I submit my review?
Once you have submitted your review, send us an email at review@theartofservice.com with the link to your review so we can properly thank you for your feedback.

Purpose of this Self-Assessment

This Self-Assessment has been developed to improve understanding of the requirements and elements of Data Center Networking, based on best practices and standards in business process architecture, design and quality management.

It is designed to allow for a rapid Self-Assessment to determine how closely existing management practices and procedures correspond to the elements of the Self-Assessment.

The criteria of requirements and elements of Data Center Networking have been rephrased in the format of a Self-Assessment questionnaire, with a seven-criterion scoring system, as explained in this document.

In this format, even with limited background knowledge of

Data Center Networking, a manager can quickly review existing operations to determine how they measure up to the standards. This in turn can serve as the starting point of a 'gap analysis' to identify management tools or system elements that might usefully be implemented in the organization to help improve overall performance.

How to use the Self-Assessment

On the following pages are a series of questions to identify to what extent your Data Center Networking initiative is complete in comparison to the requirements set in standards.

To facilitate answering the questions, there is a space in front of each question to enter a score on a scale of '1' to '5'.

1 Strongly Disagree

2 Disagree

3 Neutral

4 Agree

5 Strongly Agree

Read the question and rate it with the following in front of mind:

'In my belief,
the answer to this question is clearly defined'.

There are two ways in which you can choose to interpret this statement;
1. how aware are you that the answer to the question is clearly defined
2. for more in-depth analysis you can choose to gather

evidence and confirm the answer to the question. This obviously will take more time, most Self-Assessment users opt for the first way to interpret the question and dig deeper later on based on the outcome of the overall Self-Assessment.

A score of '1' would mean that the answer is not clear at all, where a '5' would mean the answer is crystal clear and defined. Leave emtpy when the question is not applicable or you don't want to answer it, you can skip it without affecting your score. Write your score in the space provided.

After you have responded to all the appropriate statements in each section, compute your average score for that section, using the formula provided, and round to the nearest tenth. Then transfer to the corresponding spoke in the Data Center Networking Scorecard on the second next page of the Self-Assessment.

Your completed Data Center Networking Scorecard will give you a clear presentation of which Data Center Networking areas need attention.

Data Center Networking Scorecard Example

Example of how the finalized Scorecard can look like:

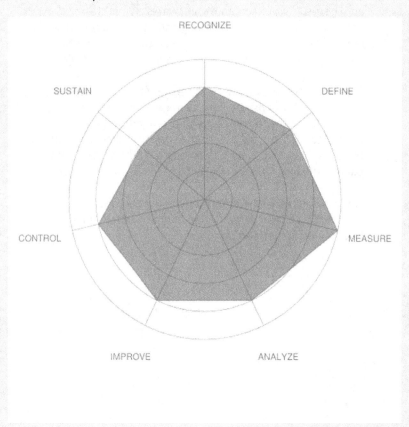

Data Center Networking Scorecard

Your Scores:

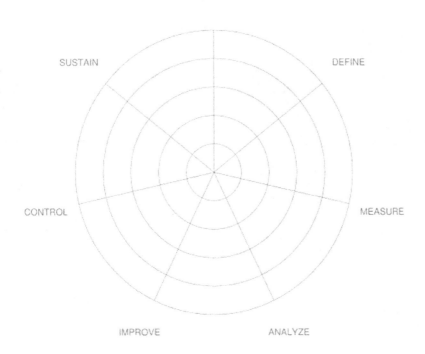

BEGINNING OF THE SELF-ASSESSMENT:

CRITERION #1: RECOGNIZE

INTENT: Be aware of the need for change. Recognize that there is an unfavorable variation, problem or symptom.

In my belief, the answer to this question is clearly defined:

5 Strongly Agree

4 Agree

3 Neutral

2 Disagree

1 Strongly Disagree

1. What is the Data Center Networking problem definition? What do you need to resolve?
<--- Score

2. What Data Center Networking problem should be solved?
<--- Score

3. Who needs budgets?

<--- Score

4. Where is training needed?
<--- Score

5. Does your organization need more Data Center Networking education?
<--- Score

6. Who else hopes to benefit from it?
<--- Score

7. Are you dealing with any of the same issues today as yesterday? What can you do about this?
<--- Score

8. Have you identified your Data Center Networking key performance indicators?
<--- Score

9. Which issues are too important to ignore?
<--- Score

10. What extra resources will you need?
<--- Score

11. What training and capacity building actions are needed to implement proposed reforms?
<--- Score

12. What does Data Center Networking success mean to the stakeholders?
<--- Score

13. For your Data Center Networking project, identify and describe the business environment, is there more

than one layer to the business environment?
<--- Score

14. What vendors make products that address the Data Center Networking needs?
<--- Score

15. How do you recognize an Data Center Networking objection?
<--- Score

16. What prevents you from making the changes you know will make you a more effective Data Center Networking leader?
<--- Score

17. To what extent does each concerned units management team recognize Data Center Networking as an effective investment?
<--- Score

18. Will Data Center Networking deliverables need to be tested and, if so, by whom?
<--- Score

19. What tools and technologies are needed for a custom Data Center Networking project?
<--- Score

20. What Data Center Networking coordination do you need?
<--- Score

21. Do you need to avoid or amend any Data Center Networking activities?
<--- Score

22. What are the minority interests and what amount of minority interests can be recognized?
<--- Score

23. Who should resolve the Data Center Networking issues?
<--- Score

24. Did you miss any major Data Center Networking issues?
<--- Score

25. Whom do you really need or want to serve?
<--- Score

26. What are the expected benefits of Data Center Networking to the stakeholder?
<--- Score

27. Is it needed?
<--- Score

28. Do you need different information or graphics?
<--- Score

29. What are the stakeholder objectives to be achieved with Data Center Networking?
<--- Score

30. What is the extent or complexity of the Data Center Networking problem?
<--- Score

31. Are there any revenue recognition issues?
<--- Score

32. What would happen if Data Center Networking weren't done?

<--- Score

33. What problems are you facing and how do you consider Data Center Networking will circumvent those obstacles?

<--- Score

34. How much are sponsors, customers, partners, stakeholders involved in Data Center Networking? In other words, what are the risks, if Data Center Networking does not deliver successfully?

<--- Score

35. Why is this needed?

<--- Score

36. Who needs to know about Data Center Networking?

<--- Score

37. How are the Data Center Networking's objectives aligned to the group's overall stakeholder strategy?

<--- Score

38. How are training requirements identified?

<--- Score

39. What else needs to be measured?

<--- Score

40. Think about the people you identified for your Data Center Networking project and the project responsibilities you would assign to them, what kind

of training do you think they would need to perform these responsibilities effectively?
<--- Score

41. Are your goals realistic? Do you need to redefine your problem? Perhaps the problem has changed or maybe you have reached your goal and need to set a new one?
<--- Score

42. What should be considered when identifying available resources, constraints, and deadlines?
<--- Score

43. As a sponsor, customer or management, how important is it to meet goals, objectives?
<--- Score

44. Are controls defined to recognize and contain problems?
<--- Score

45. What creative shifts do you need to take?
<--- Score

46. Will new equipment/products be required to facilitate Data Center Networking delivery, for example is new software needed?
<--- Score

47. Are employees recognized for desired behaviors?
<--- Score

48. What are the clients issues and concerns?
<--- Score

49. Who needs to know?
<--- Score

50. Can management personnel recognize the monetary benefit of Data Center Networking?
<--- Score

51. Who needs what information?
<--- Score

52. Do you know what you need to know about Data Center Networking?
<--- Score

53. What situation(s) led to this Data Center Networking Self Assessment?
<--- Score

54. Are there recognized Data Center Networking problems?
<--- Score

55. What is the problem and/or vulnerability?
<--- Score

56. Are there any specific expectations or concerns about the Data Center Networking team, Data Center Networking itself?
<--- Score

57. Are there Data Center Networking problems defined?
<--- Score

58. Will a response program recognize when a crisis occurs and provide some level of response?

<--- Score

59. Which needs are not included or involved?
<--- Score

60. What is the recognized need?
<--- Score

61. Who are your key stakeholders who need to sign off?
<--- Score

62. What Data Center Networking capabilities do you need?
<--- Score

63. What are the timeframes required to resolve each of the issues/problems?
<--- Score

64. What are your needs in relation to Data Center Networking skills, labor, equipment, and markets?
<--- Score

65. Consider your own Data Center Networking project, what types of organizational problems do you think might be causing or affecting your problem, based on the work done so far?
<--- Score

66. Who defines the rules in relation to any given issue?
<--- Score

67. What needs to be done?
<--- Score

68. When a Data Center Networking manager recognizes a problem, what options are available?
<--- Score

69. What are the Data Center Networking resources needed?
<--- Score

70. Are employees recognized or rewarded for performance that demonstrates the highest levels of integrity?
<--- Score

71. Do you recognize Data Center Networking achievements?
<--- Score

72. What is the smallest subset of the problem you can usefully solve?
<--- Score

73. Are problem definition and motivation clearly presented?
<--- Score

74. Would you recognize a threat from the inside?
<--- Score

75. How do you identify subcontractor relationships?
<--- Score

76. What needs to stay?
<--- Score

77. What resources or support might you need?

<--- Score

78. To what extent would your organization benefit from being recognized as a award recipient?
<--- Score

79. How do you take a forward-looking perspective in identifying Data Center Networking research related to market response and models?
<--- Score

80. How many trainings, in total, are needed?
<--- Score

81. Will it solve real problems?
<--- Score

82. How do you identify the kinds of information that you will need?
<--- Score

83. Is it clear when you think of the day ahead of you what activities and tasks you need to complete?
<--- Score

84. Why the need?
<--- Score

85. What Data Center Networking events should you attend?
<--- Score

86. Which information does the Data Center Networking business case need to include?
<--- Score

87. Are losses recognized in a timely manner?
<--- Score

88. What information do users need?
<--- Score

89. What do you need to start doing?
<--- Score

90. What is the problem or issue?
<--- Score

91. Does Data Center Networking create potential expectations in other areas that need to be recognized and considered?
<--- Score

92. Is the need for organizational change recognized?
<--- Score

93. How do you recognize an objection?
<--- Score

94. How are you going to measure success?
<--- Score

95. Are there regulatory / compliance issues?
<--- Score

96. Is the quality assurance team identified?
<--- Score

97. What activities does the governance board need to consider?
<--- Score

Add up total points for this section:
_____ = Total points for this section

Divided by: _____ (number of
statements answered) = _____
Average score for this section

Transfer your score to the Data Center
Networking Index at the beginning of
the Self-Assessment.

CRITERION #2: DEFINE:

INTENT: Formulate the stakeholder problem. Define the problem, needs and objectives.

In my belief, the answer to this question is clearly defined:

5 Strongly Agree

4 Agree

3 Neutral

2 Disagree

1 Strongly Disagree

1. Has a team charter been developed and communicated?
<--- Score

2. What intelligence can you gather?
<--- Score

3. What scope do you want your strategy to cover?
<--- Score

4. Is there a clear Data Center Networking case definition?
<--- Score

5. What sources do you use to gather information for a Data Center Networking study?
<--- Score

6. What information do you gather?
<--- Score

7. Has/have the customer(s) been identified?
<--- Score

8. What happens if Data Center Networking's scope changes?
<--- Score

9. Is the team adequately staffed with the desired cross-functionality? If not, what additional resources are available to the team?
<--- Score

10. Is Data Center Networking required?
<--- Score

11. How often are the team meetings?
<--- Score

12. What are the compelling stakeholder reasons for embarking on Data Center Networking?
<--- Score

13. If substitutes have been appointed, have they been briefed on the Data Center Networking goals

and received regular communications as to the progress to date?
<--- Score

14. Are all requirements met?
<--- Score

15. How are consistent Data Center Networking definitions important?
<--- Score

16. Has a high-level 'as is' process map been completed, verified and validated?
<--- Score

17. Are there any constraints known that bear on the ability to perform Data Center Networking work? How is the team addressing them?
<--- Score

18. Who approved the Data Center Networking scope?
<--- Score

19. Does the scope remain the same?
<--- Score

20. How will variation in the actual durations of each activity be dealt with to ensure that the expected Data Center Networking results are met?
<--- Score

21. Are approval levels defined for contracts and supplements to contracts?
<--- Score

22. What are the Roles and Responsibilities for each team member and its leadership? Where is this documented?
<--- Score

23. What key stakeholder process output measure(s) does Data Center Networking leverage and how?
<--- Score

24. What is the definition of Data Center Networking excellence?
<--- Score

25. What are the Data Center Networking use cases?
<--- Score

26. Has the direction changed at all during the course of Data Center Networking? If so, when did it change and why?
<--- Score

27. Are required metrics defined, what are they?
<--- Score

28. Is there a critical path to deliver Data Center Networking results?
<--- Score

29. What constraints exist that might impact the team?
<--- Score

30. How do you gather requirements?
<--- Score

31. How have you defined all Data Center Networking

requirements first?

<--- Score

32. What is the scope of Data Center Networking?

<--- Score

33. What Data Center Networking requirements should be gathered?

<--- Score

34. How do you gather the stories?

<--- Score

35. What system do you use for gathering Data Center Networking information?

<--- Score

36. Do the problem and goal statements meet the SMART criteria (specific, measurable, attainable, relevant, and time-bound)?

<--- Score

37. How would you define the culture at your organization, how susceptible is it to Data Center Networking changes?

<--- Score

38. When is/was the Data Center Networking start date?

<--- Score

39. Are roles and responsibilities formally defined?

<--- Score

40. What are the boundaries of the scope? What is in bounds and what is not? What is the start point? What

is the stop point?
<--- Score

41. What are the record-keeping requirements of Data Center Networking activities?
<--- Score

42. What are the tasks and definitions?
<--- Score

43. Scope of sensitive information?
<--- Score

44. What baselines are required to be defined and managed?
<--- Score

45. Is there a completed SIPOC representation, describing the Suppliers, Inputs, Process, Outputs, and Customers?
<--- Score

46. Is it clearly defined in and to your organization what you do?
<--- Score

47. Is scope creep really all bad news?
<--- Score

48. What are the rough order estimates on cost savings/opportunities that Data Center Networking brings?
<--- Score

49. Has a project plan, Gantt chart, or similar been developed/completed?

<--- Score

50. How do you catch Data Center Networking definition inconsistencies?
<--- Score

51. What are the Data Center Networking tasks and definitions?
<--- Score

52. What scope to assess?
<--- Score

53. When is the estimated completion date?
<--- Score

54. Where can you gather more information?
<--- Score

55. Why are you doing Data Center Networking and what is the scope?
<--- Score

56. What are (control) requirements for Data Center Networking Information?
<--- Score

57. Who defines (or who defined) the rules and roles?
<--- Score

58. Is the Data Center Networking scope manageable?
<--- Score

59. What is the scope of the Data Center Networking effort?
<--- Score

60. The political context: who holds power?
<--- Score

61. Is Data Center Networking linked to key stakeholder goals and objectives?
<--- Score

62. How does the Data Center Networking manager ensure against scope creep?
<--- Score

63. How and when will the baselines be defined?
<--- Score

64. What gets examined?
<--- Score

65. What is the context?
<--- Score

66. Who are the Data Center Networking improvement team members, including Management Leads and Coaches?
<--- Score

67. How will the Data Center Networking team and the group measure complete success of Data Center Networking?
<--- Score

68. What would be the goal or target for a Data Center Networking's improvement team?
<--- Score

69. In what way can you redefine the criteria of choice

clients have in your category in your favor?
<--- Score

70. What is the scope of the Data Center Networking work?
<--- Score

71. What sort of initial information to gather?
<--- Score

72. Who is gathering information?
<--- Score

73. How do you manage scope?
<--- Score

74. What critical content must be communicated – who, what, when, where, and how?
<--- Score

75. What is out of scope?
<--- Score

76. Is the improvement team aware of the different versions of a process: what they think it is vs. what it actually is vs. what it should be vs. what it could be?
<--- Score

77. Are the Data Center Networking requirements complete?
<--- Score

78. Has anyone else (internal or external to the group) attempted to solve this problem or a similar one before? If so, what knowledge can be leveraged from these previous efforts?

<--- Score

79. Have all of the relationships been defined properly?
<--- Score

80. Is the scope of Data Center Networking defined?
<--- Score

81. Are audit criteria, scope, frequency and methods defined?
<--- Score

82. Is there a completed, verified, and validated high-level 'as is' (not 'should be' or 'could be') stakeholder process map?
<--- Score

83. How do you hand over Data Center Networking context?
<--- Score

84. How is the team tracking and documenting its work?
<--- Score

85. Do you have organizational privacy requirements?
<--- Score

86. Are accountability and ownership for Data Center Networking clearly defined?
<--- Score

87. How do you manage unclear Data Center Networking requirements?
<--- Score

88. What specifically is the problem? Where does it occur? When does it occur? What is its extent?
<--- Score

89. How do you keep key subject matter experts in the loop?
<--- Score

90. Has a Data Center Networking requirement not been met?
<--- Score

91. Is the work to date meeting requirements?
<--- Score

92. What is in scope?
<--- Score

93. What are the core elements of the Data Center Networking business case?
<--- Score

94. What defines best in class?
<--- Score

95. Do you all define Data Center Networking in the same way?
<--- Score

96. Does the team have regular meetings?
<--- Score

97. Is the Data Center Networking scope complete and appropriately sized?
<--- Score

98. Are there different segments of customers?
<--- Score

99. Has the improvement team collected the 'voice of the customer' (obtained feedback – qualitative and quantitative)?
<--- Score

100. Has your scope been defined?
<--- Score

101. Is there regularly 100% attendance at the team meetings? If not, have appointed substitutes attended to preserve cross-functionality and full representation?
<--- Score

102. How do you think the partners involved in Data Center Networking would have defined success?
<--- Score

103. What are the dynamics of the communication plan?
<--- Score

104. Are task requirements clearly defined?
<--- Score

105. How was the 'as is' process map developed, reviewed, verified and validated?
<--- Score

106. Are resources adequate for the scope?
<--- Score

107. What is in the scope and what is not in scope?
<--- Score

108. Are the Data Center Networking requirements testable?
<--- Score

109. What are the requirements for audit information?
<--- Score

110. What is the definition of success?
<--- Score

111. What Data Center Networking services do you require?
<--- Score

112. What knowledge or experience is required?
<--- Score

113. How can the value of Data Center Networking be defined?
<--- Score

114. How do you build the right business case?
<--- Score

115. Have the customer needs been translated into specific, measurable requirements? How?
<--- Score

116. How did the Data Center Networking manager receive input to the development of a Data Center Networking improvement plan and the estimated completion dates/times of each activity?
<--- Score

117. Is the current 'as is' process being followed? If not, what are the discrepancies?
<--- Score

118. Are different versions of process maps needed to account for the different types of inputs?
<--- Score

119. Has everyone on the team, including the team leaders, been properly trained?
<--- Score

120. Is Data Center Networking currently on schedule according to the plan?
<--- Score

121. What is out-of-scope initially?
<--- Score

122. How do you manage changes in Data Center Networking requirements?
<--- Score

123. Have specific policy objectives been defined?
<--- Score

124. Have all basic functions of Data Center Networking been defined?
<--- Score

125. How would you define Data Center Networking leadership?
<--- Score

126. Who is gathering Data Center Networking

information?
<--- Score

127. When are meeting minutes sent out? Who is on the distribution list?
<--- Score

128. Has the Data Center Networking work been fairly and/or equitably divided and delegated among team members who are qualified and capable to perform the work? Has everyone contributed?
<--- Score

129. What customer feedback methods were used to solicit their input?
<--- Score

130. Is there any additional Data Center Networking definition of success?
<--- Score

131. Is special Data Center Networking user knowledge required?
<--- Score

Add up total points for this section:
_ _ _ _ _ = Total points for this section

Divided by: _ _ _ _ _ _ (number of statements answered) = _ _ _ _ _ _
Average score for this section

Transfer your score to the Data Center Networking Index at the beginning of the Self-Assessment.

CRITERION #3: MEASURE:

INTENT: Gather the correct data.
Measure the current performance and
evolution of the situation.

In my belief, the answer to this
question is clearly defined:

5 Strongly Agree

4 Agree

3 Neutral

2 Disagree

1 Strongly Disagree

1. Are there measurements based on task
performance?
<--- Score

2. What would it cost to replace your technology?
<--- Score

3. What measurements are possible, practicable and
meaningful?

<--- Score

4. When are costs are incurred?
<--- Score

5. How will costs be allocated?
<--- Score

6. When a disaster occurs, who gets priority?
<--- Score

7. Why a Data Center Networking focus?
<--- Score

8. Among the Data Center Networking product and service cost to be estimated, which is considered hardest to estimate?
<--- Score

9. What is the cost of rework?
<--- Score

10. What are your primary costs, revenues, assets?
<--- Score

11. What are your key Data Center Networking organizational performance measures, including key short and longer-term financial measures?
<--- Score

12. Has a cost center been established?
<--- Score

13. What are the uncertainties surrounding estimates of impact?
<--- Score

14. Have you made assumptions about the shape of the future, particularly its impact on your customers and competitors?
<--- Score

15. How can you measure the performance?
<--- Score

16. What methods are feasible and acceptable to estimate the impact of reforms?
<--- Score

17. How to cause the change?
<--- Score

18. Which costs should be taken into account?
<--- Score

19. How do you verify and develop ideas and innovations?
<--- Score

20. How do you verify the authenticity of the data and information used?
<--- Score

21. What are your customers expectations and measures?
<--- Score

22. Are missed Data Center Networking opportunities costing your organization money?
<--- Score

23. What measurements are being captured?

<--- Score

24. What is the root cause(s) of the problem?
<--- Score

25. Are you aware of what could cause a problem?
<--- Score

26. What does losing customers cost your organization?
<--- Score

27. What is measured? Why?
<--- Score

28. What are you verifying?
<--- Score

29. Did you tackle the cause or the symptom?
<--- Score

30. How frequently do you track Data Center Networking measures?
<--- Score

31. How are costs allocated?
<--- Score

32. What are the costs?
<--- Score

33. What users will be impacted?
<--- Score

34. How much does it cost?
<--- Score

35. How will measures be used to manage and adapt?
<--- Score

36. What do you measure and why?
<--- Score

37. Are actual costs in line with budgeted costs?
<--- Score

38. What are your operating costs?
<--- Score

39. What harm might be caused?
<--- Score

40. Does management have the right priorities among projects?
<--- Score

41. Do you verify that corrective actions were taken?
<--- Score

42. How can a Data Center Networking test verify your ideas or assumptions?
<--- Score

43. Do you have a flow diagram of what happens?
<--- Score

44. How will success or failure be measured?
<--- Score

45. How do you control the overall costs of your work processes?
<--- Score

46. Are you taking your company in the direction of better and revenue or cheaper and cost?
<--- Score

47. What is an unallowable cost?
<--- Score

48. How can you reduce the costs of obtaining inputs?
<--- Score

49. Are indirect costs charged to the Data Center Networking program?
<--- Score

50. What could cause delays in the schedule?
<--- Score

51. What is the Data Center Networking business impact?
<--- Score

52. How is progress measured?
<--- Score

53. What does verifying compliance entail?
<--- Score

54. How do you verify performance?
<--- Score

55. Do you aggressively reward and promote the people who have the biggest impact on creating excellent Data Center Networking services/products?
<--- Score

56. How do you measure lifecycle phases?
<--- Score

57. How frequently do you verify your Data Center Networking strategy?
<--- Score

58. What does your operating model cost?
<--- Score

59. How is performance measured?
<--- Score

60. Are the Data Center Networking benefits worth its costs?
<--- Score

61. Which measures and indicators matter?
<--- Score

62. Is it possible to estimate the impact of unanticipated complexity such as wrong or failed assumptions, feedback, etcetera on proposed reforms?
<--- Score

63. What evidence is there and what is measured?
<--- Score

64. Why do the measurements/indicators matter?
<--- Score

65. How do your measurements capture actionable Data Center Networking information for use in exceeding your customers expectations and securing your customers engagement?

<--- Score

66. What does a Test Case verify?
<--- Score

67. What do people want to verify?
<--- Score

68. What causes mismanagement?
<--- Score

69. Do you have an issue in getting priority?
<--- Score

70. How can you reduce costs?
<--- Score

71. Are there any easy-to-implement alternatives to Data Center Networking? Sometimes other solutions are available that do not require the cost implications of a full-blown project?
<--- Score

72. How do you verify Data Center Networking completeness and accuracy?
<--- Score

73. How are measurements made?
<--- Score

74. What potential environmental factors impact the Data Center Networking effort?
<--- Score

75. What drives O&M cost?
<--- Score

76. What causes investor action?
<--- Score

77. When should you bother with diagrams?
<--- Score

78. Do the benefits outweigh the costs?
<--- Score

79. Are you able to realize any cost savings?
<--- Score

80. How is the value delivered by Data Center Networking being measured?
<--- Score

81. What causes innovation to fail or succeed in your organization?
<--- Score

82. Are Data Center Networking vulnerabilities categorized and prioritized?
<--- Score

83. Are the units of measure consistent?
<--- Score

84. How will you measure your Data Center Networking effectiveness?
<--- Score

85. What are the costs of reform?
<--- Score

86. Who is involved in verifying compliance?

<--- Score

87. What relevant entities could be measured?
<--- Score

88. How long to keep data and how to manage retention costs?
<--- Score

89. How can you measure Data Center Networking in a systematic way?
<--- Score

90. Is there an opportunity to verify requirements?
<--- Score

91. What are hidden Data Center Networking quality costs?
<--- Score

92. Are the measurements objective?
<--- Score

93. How sensitive must the Data Center Networking strategy be to cost?
<--- Score

94. How do you quantify and qualify impacts?
<--- Score

95. Who pays the cost?
<--- Score

96. Do you have any cost Data Center Networking limitation requirements?
<--- Score

97. The approach of traditional Data Center Networking works for detail complexity but is focused on a systematic approach rather than an understanding of the nature of systems themselves, what approach will permit your organization to deal with the kind of unpredictable emergent behaviors that dynamic complexity can introduce?
<--- Score

98. How do you measure success?
<--- Score

99. What can be used to verify compliance?
<--- Score

100. How will your organization measure success?
<--- Score

101. What would be a real cause for concern?
<--- Score

102. What are the costs and benefits?
<--- Score

103. What are allowable costs?
<--- Score

104. Do you effectively measure and reward individual and team performance?
<--- Score

105. How do you measure efficient delivery of Data Center Networking services?
<--- Score

106. How will you measure success?
<--- Score

107. How do you verify if Data Center Networking is built right?
<--- Score

108. What is the total cost related to deploying Data Center Networking, including any consulting or professional services?
<--- Score

109. What are the Data Center Networking investment costs?
<--- Score

110. Have design-to-cost goals been established?
<--- Score

111. How do you verify and validate the Data Center Networking data?
<--- Score

112. What could cause you to change course?
<--- Score

113. Where is it measured?
<--- Score

114. Are supply costs steady or fluctuating?
<--- Score

115. What are the current costs of the Data Center Networking process?
<--- Score

116. What causes extra work or rework?
<--- Score

117. What tests verify requirements?
<--- Score

118. What are the strategic priorities for this year?
<--- Score

119. What are the Data Center Networking key cost drivers?
<--- Score

120. Are there competing Data Center Networking priorities?
<--- Score

121. What are the costs of delaying Data Center Networking action?
<--- Score

122. Where can you go to verify the info?
<--- Score

123. How do you verify your resources?
<--- Score

124. Does the Data Center Networking task fit the client's priorities?
<--- Score

125. How do you aggregate measures across priorities?
<--- Score

126. What are the estimated costs of proposed

changes?
<--- Score

127. Does a Data Center Networking quantification method exist?
<--- Score

128. Is the solution cost-effective?
<--- Score

129. Is the cost worth the Data Center Networking effort ?
<--- Score

130. Was a business case (cost/benefit) developed?
<--- Score

131. What is the total fixed cost?
<--- Score

132. Which Data Center Networking impacts are significant?
<--- Score

133. What is your Data Center Networking quality cost segregation study?
<--- Score

134. How will effects be measured?
<--- Score

135. What happens if cost savings do not materialize?
<--- Score

136. What are the types and number of measures to use?

<--- Score

137. What details are required of the Data Center Networking cost structure?
<--- Score

138. How do you verify the Data Center Networking requirements quality?
<--- Score

139. What is the cause of any Data Center Networking gaps?
<--- Score

140. How can you manage cost down?
<--- Score

Add up total points for this section:
_ _ _ _ _ = Total points for this section

Divided by: _ _ _ _ _ _ (number of statements answered) = _ _ _ _ _ _
Average score for this section

Transfer your score to the Data Center Networking Index at the beginning of the Self-Assessment.

CRITERION #4: ANALYZE:

1. How do you ensure that the Data Center Networking opportunity is realistic?
<--- Score

2. What resources go in to get the desired output?
<--- Score

3. What are the best opportunities for value improvement?
<--- Score

4. What is the complexity of the output produced?
<--- Score

5. Do quality systems drive continuous improvement?
<--- Score

6. Where is Data Center Networking data gathered?
<--- Score

7. How much data can be collected in the given timeframe?
<--- Score

8. Is there an established change management process?
<--- Score

9. What are your current levels and trends in key measures or indicators of Data Center Networking product and process performance that are important to and directly serve your customers? How do these results compare with the performance of your competitors and other organizations with similar offerings?
<--- Score

10. What are the processes for audit reporting and management?
<--- Score

11. How is the way you as the leader think and process information affecting your organizational culture?
<--- Score

12. How is the Data Center Networking Value Stream

Mapping managed?

<--- Score

13. How do mission and objectives affect the Data Center Networking processes of your organization?

<--- Score

14. Do staff qualifications match your project?

<--- Score

15. How do you use Data Center Networking data and information to support organizational decision making and innovation?

<--- Score

16. What Data Center Networking metrics are outputs of the process?

<--- Score

17. What qualifications are necessary?

<--- Score

18. Do you understand your management processes today?

<--- Score

19. What is the oversight process?

<--- Score

20. Who is involved in the management review process?

<--- Score

21. What process should you select for improvement?

<--- Score

22. Who gets your output?
<--- Score

23. Record-keeping requirements flow from the records needed as inputs, outputs, controls and for transformation of a Data Center Networking process, are the records needed as inputs to the Data Center Networking process available?
<--- Score

24. What do you need to qualify?
<--- Score

25. How do you implement and manage your work processes to ensure that they meet design requirements?
<--- Score

26. Were Pareto charts (or similar) used to portray the 'heavy hitters' (or key sources of variation)?
<--- Score

27. What are the revised rough estimates of the financial savings/opportunity for Data Center Networking improvements?
<--- Score

28. How are outputs preserved and protected?
<--- Score

29. How often will data be collected for measures?
<--- Score

30. Are Data Center Networking changes recognized early enough to be approved through the regular process?

<--- Score

31. What tools were used to generate the list of possible causes?
<--- Score

32. What are the disruptive Data Center Networking technologies that enable your organization to radically change your business processes?
<--- Score

33. Can you add value to the current Data Center Networking decision-making process (largely qualitative) by incorporating uncertainty modeling (more quantitative)?
<--- Score

34. What are your Data Center Networking processes?
<--- Score

35. How do you define collaboration and team output?
<--- Score

36. Do your leaders quickly bounce back from setbacks?
<--- Score

37. What are your best practices for minimizing Data Center Networking project risk, while demonstrating incremental value and quick wins throughout the Data Center Networking project lifecycle?
<--- Score

38. Do your employees have the opportunity to do what they do best everyday?

<--- Score

39. What is the cost of poor quality as supported by the team's analysis?
<--- Score

40. What training and qualifications will you need?
<--- Score

41. Are your outputs consistent?
<--- Score

42. What quality tools were used to get through the analyze phase?
<--- Score

43. How will the Data Center Networking data be captured?
<--- Score

44. Do you have the authority to produce the output?
<--- Score

45. How do you measure the operational performance of your key work systems and processes, including productivity, cycle time, and other appropriate measures of process effectiveness, efficiency, and innovation?
<--- Score

46. An organizationally feasible system request is one that considers the mission, goals and objectives of the organization, key questions are: is the Data Center Networking solution request practical and will it solve a problem or take advantage of an opportunity to achieve company goals?

<--- Score

47. What were the crucial 'moments of truth' on the process map?
<--- Score

48. How can architecture help to reduce energy consumption in data center networking?
<--- Score

49. How has the Data Center Networking data been gathered?
<--- Score

50. How will the change process be managed?
<--- Score

51. What, related to, Data Center Networking processes does your organization outsource?
<--- Score

52. Were there any improvement opportunities identified from the process analysis?
<--- Score

53. How does the organization define, manage, and improve its Data Center Networking processes?
<--- Score

54. What types of data do your Data Center Networking indicators require?
<--- Score

55. What tools were used to narrow the list of possible causes?
<--- Score

56. Have you defined which data is gathered how?
<--- Score

57. Has data output been validated?
<--- Score

58. What qualifications and skills do you need?
<--- Score

59. Has an output goal been set?
<--- Score

60. What qualifications are needed?
<--- Score

61. Do you, as a leader, bounce back quickly from setbacks?
<--- Score

62. Where is the data coming from to measure compliance?
<--- Score

63. Who qualifies to gain access to data?
<--- Score

64. How will the data be checked for quality?
<--- Score

65. What were the financial benefits resulting from any 'ground fruit or low-hanging fruit' (quick fixes)?
<--- Score

66. What kind of crime could a potential new hire have committed that would not only not disqualify

him/her from being hired by your organization, but would actually indicate that he/she might be a particularly good fit?
<--- Score

67. What are your key performance measures or indicators and in-process measures for the control and improvement of your Data Center Networking processes?
<--- Score

68. Who will gather what data?
<--- Score

69. Who is involved with workflow mapping?
<--- Score

70. What systems/processes must you excel at?
<--- Score

71. How do you identify specific Data Center Networking investment opportunities and emerging trends?
<--- Score

72. What methods do you use to gather Data Center Networking data?
<--- Score

73. What other organizational variables, such as reward systems or communication systems, affect the performance of this Data Center Networking process?
<--- Score

74. What other jobs or tasks affect the performance of the steps in the Data Center Networking process?

<--- Score

75. What is the Data Center Networking Driver?
<--- Score

76. What is the output?
<--- Score

77. Are all team members qualified for all tasks?
<--- Score

78. How can risk management be tied procedurally to process elements?
<--- Score

79. What information qualified as important?
<--- Score

80. Is the required Data Center Networking data gathered?
<--- Score

81. Do your contracts/agreements contain data security obligations?
<--- Score

82. What is your organizations system for selecting qualified vendors?
<--- Score

83. Who will facilitate the team and process?
<--- Score

84. Do several people in different organizational units assist with the Data Center Networking process?
<--- Score

85. Which Data Center Networking data should be retained?
<--- Score

86. What Data Center Networking data do you gather or use now?
<--- Score

87. Is there any way to speed up the process?
<--- Score

88. What internal processes need improvement?
<--- Score

89. What Data Center Networking data should be managed?
<--- Score

90. What are evaluation criteria for the output?
<--- Score

91. What are your outputs?
<--- Score

92. What qualifications do Data Center Networking leaders need?
<--- Score

93. How is the data gathered?
<--- Score

94. Where can you get qualified talent today?
<--- Score

95. Are all staff in core Data Center Networking

subjects Highly Qualified?
<--- Score

96. How will corresponding data be collected?
<--- Score

97. A compounding model resolution with available relevant data can often provide insight towards a solution methodology; which Data Center Networking models, tools and techniques are necessary?
<--- Score

98. What process improvements will be needed?
<--- Score

99. When should a process be art not science?
<--- Score

100. Were any designed experiments used to generate additional insight into the data analysis?
<--- Score

101. Should you invest in industry-recognized qualifications?
<--- Score

102. Think about the functions involved in your Data Center Networking project, what processes flow from these functions?
<--- Score

103. What successful thing are you doing today that may be blinding you to new growth opportunities?
<--- Score

104. What Data Center Networking data should be collected?
<--- Score

105. Identify an operational issue in your organization, for example, could a particular task be done more quickly or more efficiently by Data Center Networking?
<--- Score

106. What data is gathered?
<--- Score

107. Think about some of the processes you undertake within your organization, which do you own?
<--- Score

108. How many input/output points does it require?
<--- Score

109. Is there a strict change management process?
<--- Score

110. What are your current levels and trends in key Data Center Networking measures or indicators of product and process performance that are important to and directly serve your customers?
<--- Score

111. Is pre-qualification of suppliers carried out?
<--- Score

112. Is the final output clearly identified?
<--- Score

113. What is the Value Stream Mapping?
<--- Score

114. What did the team gain from developing a sub-process map?
<--- Score

115. What controls do you have in place to protect data?
<--- Score

116. What is your organizations process which leads to recognition of value generation?
<--- Score

117. What does the data say about the performance of the stakeholder process?
<--- Score

118. How does architecture help to reduce energy consumption in data center networking?
<--- Score

119. How do you promote understanding that opportunity for improvement is not criticism of the status quo, or the people who created the status quo?
<--- Score

120. Is the suppliers process defined and controlled?
<--- Score

121. What qualifies as competition?
<--- Score

122. What Data Center Networking data will be collected?

<--- Score

123. How is data used for program management and improvement?
<--- Score

124. How do your work systems and key work processes relate to and capitalize on your core competencies?
<--- Score

125. How is Data Center Networking data gathered?
<--- Score

126. What are the Data Center Networking business drivers?
<--- Score

127. Who owns what data?
<--- Score

128. How difficult is it to qualify what Data Center Networking ROI is?
<--- Score

129. What will drive Data Center Networking change?
<--- Score

130. What conclusions were drawn from the team's data collection and analysis? How did the team reach these conclusions?
<--- Score

131. What are the personnel training and qualifications required?
<--- Score

132. What are the Data Center Networking design outputs?
<--- Score

133. How does architecture help to reduce energy consumption in your data center networking?
<--- Score

Add up total points for this section:
_____ = Total points for this section

Divided by: _____ (number of statements answered) = _____
Average score for this section

Transfer your score to the Data Center Networking Index at the beginning of the Self-Assessment.

CRITERION #5: IMPROVE:

INTENT: Develop a practical solution. Innovate, establish and test the solution and to measure the results.

In my belief, the answer to this question is clearly defined:

5 Strongly Agree

4 Agree

3 Neutral

2 Disagree

1 Strongly Disagree

1. How can you better manage risk?
<--- Score

2. What assumptions are made about the solution and approach?
<--- Score

3. What is the Data Center Networking's sustainability risk?

<--- Score

4. What practices helps your organization to develop its capacity to recognize patterns?
<--- Score

5. How will you know when its improved?
<--- Score

6. What error proofing will be done to address some of the discrepancies observed in the 'as is' process?
<--- Score

7. How do you improve your likelihood of success ?
<--- Score

8. Do vendor agreements bring new compliance risk ?
<--- Score

9. Does the goal represent a desired result that can be measured?
<--- Score

10. Who will be using the results of the measurement activities?
<--- Score

11. How do you link measurement and risk?
<--- Score

12. How will you know that you have improved?
<--- Score

13. Is there any other Data Center Networking solution?
<--- Score

14. What alternative responses are available to manage risk?
<--- Score

15. Who should make the Data Center Networking decisions?
<--- Score

16. Are you assessing Data Center Networking and risk?
<--- Score

17. How do you improve Data Center Networking service perception, and satisfaction?
<--- Score

18. Is the scope clearly documented?
<--- Score

19. Are the risks fully understood, reasonable and manageable?
<--- Score

20. How do you manage and improve your Data Center Networking work systems to deliver customer value and achieve organizational success and sustainability?
<--- Score

21. Who are the Data Center Networking decision-makers?
<--- Score

22. Risk events: what are the things that could go wrong?

<--- Score

23. How does your organization evaluate strategic Data Center Networking success?
<--- Score

24. In the past few months, what is the smallest change you have made that has had the biggest positive result? What was it about that small change that produced the large return?
<--- Score

25. What are the Data Center Networking security risks?
<--- Score

26. How scalable is your Data Center Networking solution?
<--- Score

27. How do you keep improving Data Center Networking?
<--- Score

28. Why improve in the first place?
<--- Score

29. How does the team improve its work?
<--- Score

30. Are procedures documented for managing Data Center Networking risks?
<--- Score

31. What tools were most useful during the improve phase?

<--- Score

32. What lessons, if any, from a pilot were incorporated into the design of the full-scale solution?
<--- Score

33. How do you manage Data Center Networking risk?
<--- Score

34. Who manages Data Center Networking risk?
<--- Score

35. Who do you report Data Center Networking results to?
<--- Score

36. How do you improve productivity?
<--- Score

37. What tools do you use once you have decided on a Data Center Networking strategy and more importantly how do you choose?
<--- Score

38. Is the solution technically practical?
<--- Score

39. Will the controls trigger any other risks?
<--- Score

40. What risks do you need to manage?
<--- Score

41. Are risk triggers captured?
<--- Score

42. How can you improve performance?
<--- Score

43. If you could go back in time five years, what decision would you make differently? What is your best guess as to what decision you're making today you might regret five years from now?
<--- Score

44. Have you achieved Data Center Networking improvements?
<--- Score

45. Can you integrate quality management and risk management?
<--- Score

46. How do you deal with Data Center Networking risk?
<--- Score

47. For estimation problems, how do you develop an estimation statement?
<--- Score

48. Are risk management tasks balanced centrally and locally?
<--- Score

49. Who are the Data Center Networking decision makers?
<--- Score

50. Where do you need Data Center Networking improvement?
<--- Score

51. Have you identified breakpoints and/or risk tolerances that will trigger broad consideration of a potential need for intervention or modification of strategy?
<--- Score

52. Risk factors: what are the characteristics of Data Center Networking that make it risky?
<--- Score

53. Do you combine technical expertise with business knowledge and Data Center Networking Key topics include lifecycles, development approaches, requirements and how to make a business case?
<--- Score

54. Is the Data Center Networking solution sustainable?
<--- Score

55. What strategies for Data Center Networking improvement are successful?
<--- Score

56. How will you know that a change is an improvement?
<--- Score

57. What Data Center Networking improvements can be made?
<--- Score

58. How do you mitigate Data Center Networking risk?
<--- Score

59. What does the 'should be' process map/design look like?
<--- Score

60. Was a Data Center Networking charter developed?
<--- Score

61. What to do with the results or outcomes of measurements?
<--- Score

62. How do you measure risk?
<--- Score

63. Do those selected for the Data Center Networking team have a good general understanding of what Data Center Networking is all about?
<--- Score

64. Do you cover the five essential competencies: Communication, Collaboration,Innovation, Adaptability, and Leadership that improve an organizations ability to leverage the new Data Center Networking in a volatile global economy?
<--- Score

65. Who manages supplier risk management in your organization?
<--- Score

66. Who are the key stakeholders for the Data Center Networking evaluation?
<--- Score

67. Where do the Data Center Networking decisions reside?

<--- Score

68. Is there a high likelihood that any recommendations will achieve their intended results?
<--- Score

69. How do the Data Center Networking results compare with the performance of your competitors and other organizations with similar offerings?
<--- Score

70. How do you decide how much to remunerate an employee?
<--- Score

71. How is continuous improvement applied to risk management?
<--- Score

72. To what extent does management recognize Data Center Networking as a tool to increase the results?
<--- Score

73. What current systems have to be understood and/ or changed?
<--- Score

74. Risk Identification: What are the possible risk events your organization faces in relation to Data Center Networking?
<--- Score

75. How will you measure the results?
<--- Score

76. Is Data Center Networking documentation

maintained?
<--- Score

77. Do you have the optimal project management team structure?
<--- Score

78. Are the most efficient solutions problem-specific?
<--- Score

79. How do you measure progress and evaluate training effectiveness?
<--- Score

80. What is the risk?
<--- Score

81. How is knowledge sharing about risk management improved?
<--- Score

82. Do you need to do a usability evaluation?
<--- Score

83. Is the Data Center Networking documentation thorough?
<--- Score

84. What do you want to improve?
<--- Score

85. What are the implications of the one critical Data Center Networking decision 10 minutes, 10 months, and 10 years from now?
<--- Score

86. What criteria will you use to assess your Data Center Networking risks?
<--- Score

87. Which Data Center Networking solution is appropriate?
<--- Score

88. When you map the key players in your own work and the types/domains of relationships with them, which relationships do you find easy and which challenging, and why?
<--- Score

89. How are Data Center Networking risks managed?
<--- Score

90. Would you develop a Data Center Networking Communication Strategy?
<--- Score

91. What tools were used to evaluate the potential solutions?
<--- Score

92. Was a pilot designed for the proposed solution(s)?
<--- Score

93. Were any criteria developed to assist the team in testing and evaluating potential solutions?
<--- Score

94. What improvements have been achieved?
<--- Score

95. What attendant changes will need to be made to

ensure that the solution is successful?
<--- Score

96. What tools were used to tap into the creativity and encourage 'outside the box' thinking?
<--- Score

97. What is the magnitude of the improvements?
<--- Score

98. How risky is your organization?
<--- Score

99. What communications are necessary to support the implementation of the solution?
<--- Score

100. What is Data Center Networking's impact on utilizing the best solution(s)?
<--- Score

101. What is the team's contingency plan for potential problems occurring in implementation?
<--- Score

102. Who will be responsible for making the decisions to include or exclude requested changes once Data Center Networking is underway?
<--- Score

103. What are your current levels and trends in key measures or indicators of workforce and leader development?
<--- Score

104. How can you improve Data Center Networking?

<--- Score

105. At what point will vulnerability assessments be performed once Data Center Networking is put into production (e.g., ongoing Risk Management after implementation)?
<--- Score

106. Who makes the Data Center Networking decisions in your organization?
<--- Score

107. What resources are required for the improvement efforts?
<--- Score

108. Can the solution be designed and implemented within an acceptable time period?
<--- Score

109. What are the expected Data Center Networking results?
<--- Score

110. Which of the recognised risks out of all risks can be most likely transferred?
<--- Score

111. Can you identify any significant risks or exposures to Data Center Networking third- parties (vendors, service providers, alliance partners etc) that concern you?
<--- Score

112. Are the key business and technology risks being managed?

<--- Score

113. How are policy decisions made and where?
<--- Score

114. Who controls key decisions that will be made?
<--- Score

115. Are events managed to resolution?
<--- Score

116. Does a good decision guarantee a good outcome?
<--- Score

117. What area needs the greatest improvement?
<--- Score

118. What can you do to improve?
<--- Score

119. Data Center Networking risk decisions: whose call Is It?
<--- Score

120. Is supporting Data Center Networking documentation required?
<--- Score

121. What were the underlying assumptions on the cost-benefit analysis?
<--- Score

122. What actually has to improve and by how much?
<--- Score

123. For decision problems, how do you develop a decision statement?
<--- Score

124. What is Data Center Networking risk?
<--- Score

125. What are the affordable Data Center Networking risks?
<--- Score

126. Who are the people involved in developing and implementing Data Center Networking?
<--- Score

127. What needs improvement? Why?
<--- Score

128. Is the Data Center Networking risk managed?
<--- Score

129. How can skill-level changes improve Data Center Networking?
<--- Score

130. How significant is the improvement in the eyes of the end user?
<--- Score

131. Is any Data Center Networking documentation required?
<--- Score

132. Explorations of the frontiers of Data Center Networking will help you build influence, improve Data Center Networking, optimize decision making,

and sustain change, what is your approach?
<--- Score

133. What is the implementation plan?
<--- Score

134. Are decisions made in a timely manner?
<--- Score

135. Is the measure of success for Data Center Networking understandable to a variety of people?
<--- Score

136. What should a proof of concept or pilot accomplish?
<--- Score

137. What are the concrete Data Center Networking results?
<--- Score

138. How will you recognize and celebrate results?
<--- Score

139. How can the phases of Data Center Networking development be identified?
<--- Score

140. Who controls the risk?
<--- Score

Add up total points for this section:
_ _ _ _ _ = Total points for this section

Divided by: _ _ _ _ _ _ (number of statements answered) = _ _ _ _ _ _

Average score for this section

Transfer your score to the Data Center
Networking Index at the beginning of
the Self-Assessment.

CRITERION #6: CONTROL:

INTENT: Implement the practical solution. Maintain the performance and correct possible complications.

In my belief, the answer to this question is clearly defined:

5 Strongly Agree

4 Agree

3 Neutral

2 Disagree

1 Strongly Disagree

1. How will the day-to-day responsibilities for monitoring and continual improvement be transferred from the improvement team to the process owner?
<--- Score

2. Have new or revised work instructions resulted?
<--- Score

3. How is change control managed?
<--- Score

4. How do you plan on providing proper recognition and disclosure of supporting companies?
<--- Score

5. Who is the Data Center Networking process owner?
<--- Score

6. Will any special training be provided for results interpretation?
<--- Score

7. Will existing staff require re-training, for example, to learn new business processes?
<--- Score

8. Where do ideas that reach policy makers and planners as proposals for Data Center Networking strengthening and reform actually originate?
<--- Score

9. You may have created your quality measures at a time when you lacked resources, technology wasn't up to the required standard, or low service levels were the industry norm. Have those circumstances changed?
<--- Score

10. Is there a Data Center Networking Communication plan covering who needs to get what information when?
<--- Score

11. What should the next improvement project be

that is related to Data Center Networking?
<--- Score

12. What is the recommended frequency of auditing?
<--- Score

13. What are the critical parameters to watch?
<--- Score

14. Does the Data Center Networking performance meet the customer's requirements?
<--- Score

15. What is the best design framework for Data Center Networking organization now that, in a post industrial-age if the top-down, command and control model is no longer relevant?
<--- Score

16. Will the team be available to assist members in planning investigations?
<--- Score

17. How might the group capture best practices and lessons learned so as to leverage improvements?
<--- Score

18. What are the known security controls?
<--- Score

19. Are documented procedures clear and easy to follow for the operators?
<--- Score

20. How widespread is its use?
<--- Score

21. How will new or emerging customer needs/requirements be checked/communicated to orient the process toward meeting the new specifications and continually reducing variation?
<--- Score

22. Is knowledge gained on process shared and institutionalized?
<--- Score

23. What is the control/monitoring plan?
<--- Score

24. Who has control over resources?
<--- Score

25. Does job training on the documented procedures need to be part of the process team's education and training?
<--- Score

26. What are customers monitoring?
<--- Score

27. Is the Data Center Networking test/monitoring cost justified?
<--- Score

28. Is there a control plan in place for sustaining improvements (short and long-term)?
<--- Score

29. Is there a transfer of ownership and knowledge to process owner and process team tasked with the responsibilities.

<--- Score

30. Are new process steps, standards, and documentation ingrained into normal operations?
<--- Score

31. What are the performance and scale of the Data Center Networking tools?
<--- Score

32. How will you measure your QA plan's effectiveness?
<--- Score

33. What should you measure to verify efficiency gains?
<--- Score

34. How will report readings be checked to effectively monitor performance?
<--- Score

35. What can you control?
<--- Score

36. Is new knowledge gained imbedded in the response plan?
<--- Score

37. Who sets the Data Center Networking standards?
<--- Score

38. How will input, process, and output variables be checked to detect for sub-optimal conditions?
<--- Score

39. Who is going to spread your message?
<--- Score

40. What other systems, operations, processes, and infrastructures (hiring practices, staffing, training, incentives/rewards, metrics/dashboards/scorecards, etc.) need updates, additions, changes, or deletions in order to facilitate knowledge transfer and improvements?
<--- Score

41. Are there documented procedures?
<--- Score

42. Is there a recommended audit plan for routine surveillance inspections of Data Center Networking's gains?
<--- Score

43. What are you attempting to measure/monitor?
<--- Score

44. Is a response plan established and deployed?
<--- Score

45. How do you encourage people to take control and responsibility?
<--- Score

46. Does the response plan contain a definite closed loop continual improvement scheme (e.g., plan-do-check-act)?
<--- Score

47. How will the process owner and team be able to hold the gains?

<--- Score

48. Is there an action plan in case of emergencies?
<--- Score

49. Are you measuring, monitoring and predicting Data Center Networking activities to optimize operations and profitability, and enhancing outcomes?
<--- Score

50. Does Data Center Networking appropriately measure and monitor risk?
<--- Score

51. How will the process owner verify improvement in present and future sigma levels, process capabilities?
<--- Score

52. Is a response plan in place for when the input, process, or output measures indicate an 'out-of-control' condition?
<--- Score

53. Do the viable solutions scale to future needs?
<--- Score

54. Do you monitor the Data Center Networking decisions made and fine tune them as they evolve?
<--- Score

55. What Data Center Networking standards are applicable?
<--- Score

56. How can you best use all of your knowledge

repositories to enhance learning and sharing?
<--- Score

57. What quality tools were useful in the control phase?
<--- Score

58. Is there documentation that will support the successful operation of the improvement?
<--- Score

59. How do you select, collect, align, and integrate Data Center Networking data and information for tracking daily operations and overall organizational performance, including progress relative to strategic objectives and action plans?
<--- Score

60. How do you monitor usage and cost?
<--- Score

61. Has the improved process and its steps been standardized?
<--- Score

62. Act/Adjust: What Do you Need to Do Differently?
<--- Score

63. Can support from partners be adjusted?
<--- Score

64. Does a troubleshooting guide exist or is it needed?
<--- Score

65. Are pertinent alerts monitored, analyzed and distributed to appropriate personnel?

<--- Score

66. What do you stand for--and what are you against?
<--- Score

67. How will Data Center Networking decisions be made and monitored?
<--- Score

68. Are operating procedures consistent?
<--- Score

69. Is there a standardized process?
<--- Score

70. Are the Data Center Networking standards challenging?
<--- Score

71. Who controls critical resources?
<--- Score

72. Can you adapt and adjust to changing Data Center Networking situations?
<--- Score

73. Are suggested corrective/restorative actions indicated on the response plan for known causes to problems that might surface?
<--- Score

74. Are controls in place and consistently applied?
<--- Score

75. How do you plan for the cost of succession?
<--- Score

76. Who will be in control?
<--- Score

77. How do you establish and deploy modified action plans if circumstances require a shift in plans and rapid execution of new plans?
<--- Score

78. Is there a documented and implemented monitoring plan?
<--- Score

79. Are the planned controls working?
<--- Score

80. What is your plan to assess your security risks?
<--- Score

81. Has the Data Center Networking value of standards been quantified?
<--- Score

82. Against what alternative is success being measured?
<--- Score

83. What is the standard for acceptable Data Center Networking performance?
<--- Score

84. What other areas of the group might benefit from the Data Center Networking team's improvements, knowledge, and learning?
<--- Score

85. How do controls support value?
<--- Score

86. What are the key elements of your Data Center Networking performance improvement system, including your evaluation, organizational learning, and innovation processes?
<--- Score

87. Is reporting being used or needed?
<--- Score

88. In the case of a Data Center Networking project, the criteria for the audit derive from implementation objectives, an audit of a Data Center Networking project involves assessing whether the recommendations outlined for implementation have been met, can you track that any Data Center Networking project is implemented as planned, and is it working?
<--- Score

89. How do you spread information?
<--- Score

90. What key inputs and outputs are being measured on an ongoing basis?
<--- Score

91. Do the Data Center Networking decisions you make today help people and the planet tomorrow?
<--- Score

92. Implementation Planning: is a pilot needed to test the changes before a full roll out occurs?
<--- Score

93. What do you measure to verify effectiveness gains?
<--- Score

Add up total points for this section:
_ _ _ _ _ = Total points for this section

Divided by: _ _ _ _ _ _ (number of statements answered) = _ _ _ _ _ _
Average score for this section

Transfer your score to the Data Center Networking Index at the beginning of the Self-Assessment.

CRITERION #7: SUSTAIN:

INTENT: Retain the benefits.

In my belief, the answer to this
question is clearly defined:

5 Strongly Agree

4 Agree

3 Neutral

2 Disagree

1 Strongly Disagree

1. Who are the key stakeholders?
<--- Score

2. What counts that you are not counting?
<--- Score

3. If you were responsible for initiating and
implementing major changes in your organization,
what steps might you take to ensure acceptance of
those changes?
<--- Score

4. What is an unauthorized commitment?
<--- Score

5. How will you motivate the stakeholders with the least vested interest?
<--- Score

6. Are assumptions made in Data Center Networking stated explicitly?
<--- Score

7. What stupid rule would you most like to kill?
<--- Score

8. To whom do you add value?
<--- Score

9. What information is critical to your organization that your executives are ignoring?
<--- Score

10. What are internal and external Data Center Networking relations?
<--- Score

11. How do you transition from the baseline to the target?
<--- Score

12. Why is it important to have senior management support for a Data Center Networking project?
<--- Score

13. Who are your customers?
<--- Score

14. What may be the consequences for the performance of an organization if all stakeholders are not consulted regarding Data Center Networking?
<--- Score

15. Are you / should you be revolutionary or evolutionary?
<--- Score

16. What are you trying to prove to yourself, and how might it be hijacking your life and business success?
<--- Score

17. Will your goals reflect your program budget?
<--- Score

18. Who else should you help?
<--- Score

19. What are your personal philosophies regarding Data Center Networking and how do they influence your work?
<--- Score

20. What is the range of capabilities?
<--- Score

21. What is something you believe that nearly no one agrees with you on?
<--- Score

22. How do you determine the key elements that affect Data Center Networking workforce satisfaction, how are these elements determined for different workforce groups and segments?

<--- Score

23. What is the source of the strategies for Data Center Networking strengthening and reform?
<--- Score

24. How do you keep the momentum going?
<--- Score

25. What goals did you miss?
<--- Score

26. How do you ensure that implementations of Data Center Networking products are done in a way that ensures safety?
<--- Score

27. Which models, tools and techniques are necessary?
<--- Score

28. What is the overall business strategy?
<--- Score

29. Who is responsible for Data Center Networking?
<--- Score

30. What is the craziest thing you can do?
<--- Score

31. Is there any reason to believe the opposite of my current belief?
<--- Score

32. What did you miss in the interview for the worst hire you ever made?

<--- Score

33. Why will customers want to buy your organizations products/services?
<--- Score

34. What is your BATNA (best alternative to a negotiated agreement)?
<--- Score

35. What Data Center Networking skills are most important?
<--- Score

36. Will it be accepted by users?
<--- Score

37. What are the barriers to increased Data Center Networking production?
<--- Score

38. What are the short and long-term Data Center Networking goals?
<--- Score

39. What have you done to protect your business from competitive encroachment?
<--- Score

40. Who is responsible for errors?
<--- Score

41. What is the purpose of Data Center Networking in relation to the mission?
<--- Score

42. How do you engage the workforce, in addition to satisfying them?
<--- Score

43. How do you make it meaningful in connecting Data Center Networking with what users do day-to-day?
<--- Score

44. If you do not follow, then how to lead?
<--- Score

45. What happens at your organization when people fail?
<--- Score

46. What are the long-term Data Center Networking goals?
<--- Score

47. What is the estimated value of the project?
<--- Score

48. Operational - will it work?
<--- Score

49. What are your most important goals for the strategic Data Center Networking objectives?
<--- Score

50. Will there be any necessary staff changes (redundancies or new hires)?
<--- Score

51. In a project to restructure Data Center Networking outcomes, which stakeholders would you involve?

<--- Score

52. Why not do Data Center Networking?
<--- Score

53. Are all key stakeholders present at all Structured Walkthroughs?
<--- Score

54. How do customers see your organization?
<--- Score

55. What are strategies for increasing support and reducing opposition?
<--- Score

56. What was the last experiment you ran?
<--- Score

57. Where can you break convention?
<--- Score

58. How do you lead with Data Center Networking in mind?
<--- Score

59. What are the rules and assumptions your industry operates under? What if the opposite were true?
<--- Score

60. How do you track customer value, profitability or financial return, organizational success, and sustainability?
<--- Score

61. If you had to rebuild your organization without

any traditional competitive advantages (i.e., no killer technology, promising research, innovative product/ service delivery model, etcetera), how would your people have to approach their work and collaborate together in order to create the necessary conditions for success?
<--- Score

62. How important is Data Center Networking to the user organizations mission?
<--- Score

63. How do you set Data Center Networking stretch targets and how do you get people to not only participate in setting these stretch targets but also that they strive to achieve these?
<--- Score

64. Is Data Center Networking realistic, or are you setting yourself up for failure?
<--- Score

65. Who do you want your customers to become?
<--- Score

66. What are the key enablers to make this Data Center Networking move?
<--- Score

67. Do you have past Data Center Networking successes?
<--- Score

68. Ask yourself: how would you do this work if you only had one staff member to do it?
<--- Score

69. How do you foster innovation?
<--- Score

70. What is a feasible sequencing of reform initiatives over time?
<--- Score

71. What role does communication play in the success or failure of a Data Center Networking project?
<--- Score

72. Why do and why don't your customers like your organization?
<--- Score

73. What must you excel at?
<--- Score

74. Whose voice (department, ethnic group, women, older workers, etc) might you have missed hearing from in your company, and how might you amplify this voice to create positive momentum for your business?
<--- Score

75. Why is Data Center Networking important for you now?
<--- Score

76. Who is on the team?
<--- Score

77. What is the recommended frequency of auditing?
<--- Score

78. Who have you, as a company, historically been when you've been at your best?
<--- Score

79. What are the top 3 things at the forefront of your Data Center Networking agendas for the next 3 years?
<--- Score

80. What business benefits will Data Center Networking goals deliver if achieved?
<--- Score

81. What unique value proposition (UVP) do you offer?
<--- Score

82. Which functions and people interact with the supplier and or customer?
<--- Score

83. What should you stop doing?
<--- Score

84. Can you do all this work?
<--- Score

85. When information truly is ubiquitous, when reach and connectivity are completely global, when computing resources are infinite, and when a whole new set of impossibilities are not only possible, but happening, what will that do to your business?
<--- Score

86. Who do we want your customers to become?
<--- Score

87. What is the funding source for this project?

<--- Score

88. Can the schedule be done in the given time?
<--- Score

89. What will be the consequences to the stakeholder (financial, reputation etc) if Data Center Networking does not go ahead or fails to deliver the objectives?
<--- Score

90. What are the business goals Data Center Networking is aiming to achieve?
<--- Score

91. What are you challenging?
<--- Score

92. What potential megatrends could make your business model obsolete?
<--- Score

93. Think of your Data Center Networking project, what are the main functions?
<--- Score

94. How long will it take to change?
<--- Score

95. Are the criteria for selecting recommendations stated?
<--- Score

96. Who will determine interim and final deadlines?
<--- Score

97. What management system can you use to

leverage the Data Center Networking experience, ideas, and concerns of the people closest to the work to be done?
<--- Score

98. What have been your experiences in defining long range Data Center Networking goals?
<--- Score

99. How do you foster the skills, knowledge, talents, attributes, and characteristics you want to have?
<--- Score

100. Are you making progress, and are you making progress as Data Center Networking leaders?
<--- Score

101. Is there a work around that you can use?
<--- Score

102. Is it economical; do you have the time and money?
<--- Score

103. How do you provide a safe environment -physically and emotionally?
<--- Score

104. Do you think you know, or do you know you know ?
<--- Score

105. What knowledge, skills and characteristics mark a good Data Center Networking project manager?
<--- Score

106. What would have to be true for the option on the table to be the best possible choice?
<--- Score

107. Who are four people whose careers you have enhanced?
<--- Score

108. Which Data Center Networking goals are the most important?
<--- Score

109. What does your signature ensure?
<--- Score

110. How is implementation research currently incorporated into each of your goals?
<--- Score

111. Is there any existing Data Center Networking governance structure?
<--- Score

112. How do you know if you are successful?
<--- Score

113. What relationships among Data Center Networking trends do you perceive?
<--- Score

114. Whom among your colleagues do you trust, and for what?
<--- Score

115. Political -is anyone trying to undermine this project?

<--- Score

116. What are the challenges?
<--- Score

117. How can you incorporate support to ensure safe and effective use of Data Center Networking into the services that you provide?
<--- Score

118. Can you maintain your growth without detracting from the factors that have contributed to your success?
<--- Score

119. Marketing budgets are tighter, consumers are more skeptical, and social media has changed forever the way we talk about Data Center Networking, how do you gain traction?
<--- Score

120. What projects are going on in the organization today, and what resources are those projects using from the resource pools?
<--- Score

121. What one word do you want to own in the minds of your customers, employees, and partners?
<--- Score

122. How do you proactively clarify deliverables and Data Center Networking quality expectations?
<--- Score

123. Who will provide the final approval of Data Center Networking deliverables?

<--- Score

124. Who, on the executive team or the board, has spoken to a customer recently?
<--- Score

125. What is your question? Why?
<--- Score

126. What you are going to do to affect the numbers?
<--- Score

127. What is it like to work for you?
<--- Score

128. Why should people listen to you?
<--- Score

129. Would you rather sell to knowledgeable and informed customers or to uninformed customers?
<--- Score

130. Is Data Center Networking dependent on the successful delivery of a current project?
<--- Score

131. How do you govern and fulfill your societal responsibilities?
<--- Score

132. What happens if you do not have enough funding?
<--- Score

133. How do you accomplish your long range Data Center Networking goals?

<--- Score

134. Are the assumptions believable and achievable?
<--- Score

135. How do you deal with Data Center Networking changes?
<--- Score

136. Who do you think the world wants your organization to be?
<--- Score

137. What is your Data Center Networking strategy?
<--- Score

138. Which individuals, teams or departments will be involved in Data Center Networking?
<--- Score

139. Is your basic point _____ or _____?
<--- Score

140. Who will be responsible for deciding whether Data Center Networking goes ahead or not after the initial investigations?
<--- Score

141. What new services of functionality will be implemented next with Data Center Networking ?
<--- Score

142. How will you insure seamless interoperability of Data Center Networking moving forward?
<--- Score

143. What are current Data Center Networking paradigms?
<--- Score

144. At what moment would you think; Will I get fired?
<--- Score

145. Do you have the right capabilities and capacities?
<--- Score

146. What are specific Data Center Networking rules to follow?
<--- Score

147. Who is the main stakeholder, with ultimate responsibility for driving Data Center Networking forward?
<--- Score

148. Who uses your product in ways you never expected?
<--- Score

149. What trophy do you want on your mantle?
<--- Score

150. How do you create buy-in?
<--- Score

151. What is the overall talent health of your organization as a whole at senior levels, and for each organization reporting to a member of the Senior Leadership Team?
<--- Score

152. How do you keep records, of what?

<--- Score

153. What happens when a new employee joins the organization?
<--- Score

154. How are you doing compared to your industry?
<--- Score

155. How do senior leaders deploy your organizations vision and values through your leadership system, to the workforce, to key suppliers and partners, and to customers and other stakeholders, as appropriate?
<--- Score

156. How do you go about securing Data Center Networking?
<--- Score

157. What are the gaps in your knowledge and experience?
<--- Score

158. Do you feel that more should be done in the Data Center Networking area?
<--- Score

159. How do you manage Data Center Networking Knowledge Management (KM)?
<--- Score

160. What Data Center Networking modifications can you make work for you?
<--- Score

161. Are you maintaining a past–present–future

perspective throughout the Data Center Networking discussion?
<--- Score

162. What trouble can you get into?
<--- Score

163. Do you think Data Center Networking accomplishes the goals you expect it to accomplish?
<--- Score

164. How do you listen to customers to obtain actionable information?
<--- Score

165. Who is responsible for ensuring appropriate resources (time, people and money) are allocated to Data Center Networking?
<--- Score

166. How do you maintain Data Center Networking's Integrity?
<--- Score

167. Is maximizing Data Center Networking protection the same as minimizing Data Center Networking loss?
<--- Score

Add up total points for this section:
_ _ _ _ _ = Total points for this section

Divided by: _ _ _ _ _ _ (number of statements answered) = _ _ _ _ _ _
Average score for this section

Transfer your score to the Data Center
Networking Index at the beginning of
the Self-Assessment.

Data Center Networking and Managing Projects, Criteria for Project Managers:

1.0 Initiating Process Group: Data Center Networking

1. What are the inputs required to produce the deliverables?

2. How do you help others satisfy needs?

3. How will you know you did it?

4. How should needs be met?

5. Have requirements been tested, approved, and fulfill the Data Center Networking project scope?

6. How well did the chosen processes fit the needs of the Data Center Networking project?

7. During which stage of Risk planning are risks prioritized based on probability and impact?

8. What do they need to know about the Data Center Networking project?

9. Do you know the roles & responsibilities required for this Data Center Networking project?

10. What were things that you did well, and could improve, and how?

11. Are there resources to maintain and support the outcome of the Data Center Networking project?

12. What communication items need improvement?

13. Mitigate. what will you do to minimize the impact should the risk event occur?

14. What business situation is being addressed?

15. Do you know the Data Center Networking projects goal, purpose and objectives?

16. How will you do it?

17. Does the Data Center Networking project team have enough people to execute the Data Center Networking project plan?

18. What is the stake of others in your Data Center Networking project?

19. What were things that you did very well and want to do the same again on the next Data Center Networking project?

20. What will be the pressing issues of tomorrow?

1.1 Project Charter: Data Center Networking

21. Who manages integration?

22. When?

23. Review the general mission What system will be affected by the improvement efforts?

24. Why is it important?

25. Why do you need to manage scope?

26. For whom?

27. How much?

28. What is the purpose of the Data Center Networking project?

29. What changes can you make to improve?

30. Major high-level milestone targets: what events measure progress?

31. Who ise input and support will this Data Center Networking project require?

32. Who is the Data Center Networking project Manager?

33. Who will take notes, document decisions?

34. What outcome, in measureable terms, are you hoping to accomplish?

35. Why the improvements?

36. Why have you chosen the aim you have set forth?

37. What is the justification?

38. What are the assumptions?

39. What date will the task finish?

1.2 Stakeholder Register: Data Center Networking

40. How big is the gap?

41. What opportunities exist to provide communications?

42. What is the power of the stakeholder?

43. What & Why?

44. Who are the stakeholders?

45. How much influence do they have on the Data Center Networking project?

46. How will reports be created?

47. Is your organization ready for change?

48. Who is managing stakeholder engagement?

49. How should employers make voices heard?

50. What are the major Data Center Networking project milestones requiring communications or providing communications opportunities?

51. Who wants to talk about Security?

1.3 Stakeholder Analysis Matrix: Data Center Networking

52. How affected by the problem(s)?

53. Who is most dependent on the resources at stake?

54. Who is influential in the Data Center Networking project area (both thematic and geographic areas)?

55. Resource providers; who can provide resources to ensure the implementation of the Data Center Networking project?

56. Market developments?

57. What do people from other organizations see as your organizations weaknesses?

58. What makes a person a stakeholder?

59. Who is most interested in information about the topic and/or has previously initiated interest?

60. Arena: in what fields are the actors active, where are they present?

61. Technology development and innovation?

62. Is there evidence that demonstrates the impact of education on the Data Center Networking projects outcomes?

63. Has there been a similar initiative in the region?

64. Why involve the stakeholder?

65. Who will be responsible for managing the outcome?

66. Volumes, production, economies?

67. Could any of your organizations weaknesses seriously threaten development?

68. Who will be affected by the work?

69. Who holds positions of responsibility in interested organizations?

70. What obstacles does your organization face?

71. Economy - home, abroad?

2.0 Planning Process Group: Data Center Networking

72. What is the NEXT thing to do?

73. Data Center Networking project assessment; why did you do this Data Center Networking project?

74. If task x starts two days late, what is the effect on the Data Center Networking project end date?

75. What should you do next?

76. Mitigate. what will you do to minimize the impact should a risk event occur?

77. Just how important is your work to the overall success of the Data Center Networking project?

78. Why do it Data Center Networking projects fail?

79. Are the follow-up indicators relevant and do they meet the quality needed to measure the outputs and outcomes of the Data Center Networking project?

80. To what extent are the visions and actions of the partners consistent or divergent with regard to the program?

81. To what extent has a PMO contributed to raising the quality of the design of the Data Center Networking project?

82. How well did the chosen processes fit the needs of the Data Center Networking project?

83. In which Data Center Networking project management process group is the detailed Data Center Networking project budget created?

84. Contingency planning. if a risk event occurs, what will you do?

85. Does the program have follow-up mechanisms (to verify the quality of the products, punctuality of delivery, etc.) to measure progress in the achievement of the envisaged results?

86. How can you tell when you are done?

87. In what way has the program contributed towards the issue culture and development included on the public agenda?

88. What will you do?

89. How well will the chosen processes produce the expected results?

90. What is the difference between the early schedule and late schedule?

2.1 Project Management Plan: Data Center Networking

91. What are the deliverables?

92. How do you organize the costs in the Data Center Networking project management plan?

93. If the Data Center Networking project management plan is a comprehensive document that guides you in Data Center Networking project execution and control, then what should it NOT contain?

94. What does management expect of PMs?

95. Will you add a schedule and diagram?

96. Is the budget realistic?

97. Are cost risk analysis methods applied to develop contingencies for the estimated total Data Center Networking project costs?

98. Is there anything you would now do differently on your Data Center Networking project based on past experience?

99. What if, for example, the positive direction and vision of your organization causes expected trends to change resulting in greater need than expected?

100. What went right?

101. What went wrong?

102. What happened during the process that you found interesting?

103. Are there any scope changes proposed for a previously authorized Data Center Networking project?

104. What is risk management?

105. Do there need to be organizational changes?

106. Is mitigation authorized or recommended?

107. Does the implementation plan have an appropriate division of responsibilities?

108. Do the proposed changes from the Data Center Networking project include any significant risks to safety?

109. What should you drop in order to add something new?

110. Are there any Client staffing expectations?

2.2 Scope Management Plan: Data Center Networking

111. Have all necessary approvals been obtained?

112. Given the scope of the Data Center Networking project, which criterion should be optimized?

113. Is there a formal set of procedures supporting Stakeholder Management?

114. Have the procedures for identifying variances from estimates & adjusting the detailed work program been followed?

115. Are trade-offs between accepting the risk and mitigating the risk identified?

116. What are the risks that could significantly affect the scope of the Data Center Networking project?

117. What strengths do you have?

118. Are changes in deliverable commitments agreed to by all affected groups & individuals?

119. What are the risks that could significantly affect the resources needed for the Data Center Networking project?

120. Are funding resource estimates sufficiently detailed and documented for use in planning and tracking the Data Center Networking project?

121. What are the risks that could significantly affect the communication on the Data Center Networking project?

122. Have key stakeholders been identified?

123. Are risk triggers captured?

124. Is there a scope management plan that includes how Data Center Networking project scope will be defined, developed, monitored, validated and controlled?

125. Are tasks tracked by hours?

126. Is the communication plan being followed?

127. Is there a set of procedures defining the scope, procedures, and deliverables defining quality control?

128. Has the Data Center Networking project approach and development strategy of the Data Center Networking project been defined, documented and accepted by the appropriate stakeholders?

129. Have all documents been archived in a Data Center Networking project repository for each release?

2.3 Requirements Management Plan: Data Center Networking

130. Did you provide clear and concise specifications?

131. Subject to change control?

132. Who came up with this requirement?

133. How often will the reporting occur?

134. Is there formal agreement on who has authority to approve a change in requirements?

135. Controlling Data Center Networking project requirements involves monitoring the status of the Data Center Networking project requirements and managing changes to the requirements. Who is responsible for monitoring and tracking the Data Center Networking project requirements?

136. The wbs is developed as part of a joint planning session. and how do you know that youhave done this right?

137. Is it new or replacing an existing business system or process?

138. What information regarding the Data Center Networking project requirements will be reported?

139. Are all the stakeholders ready for the transition into the user community?

140. How will you communicate scheduled tasks to other team members?

141. How will you develop the schedule of requirements activities?

142. What are you counting on?

143. Do you know which stakeholders will participate in the requirements effort?

144. Is the system software (non-operating system) new to the IT Data Center Networking project team?

145. Who will perform the analysis?

146. Do you have price sheets and a methodology for determining the total proposal cost?

147. Define the help desk model. who will take full responsibility?

148. Will the Data Center Networking project requirements become approved in writing?

149. What are you trying to do?

2.4 Requirements Documentation: Data Center Networking

150. What is effective documentation?

151. What kind of entity is a problem ?

152. Do technical resources exist?

153. Is new technology needed?

154. How will requirements be documented and who signs off on them?

155. Completeness. are all functions required by the customer included?

156. If applicable; are there issues linked with the fact that this is an offshore Data Center Networking project?

157. What will be the integration problems?

158. How does what is being described meet the business need?

159. Have the benefits identified with the system being identified clearly?

160. Who provides requirements?

161. How will the proposed Data Center Networking project help?

162. What is your Elevator Speech?

163. How do you get the user to tell you what they want?

164. What variations exist for a process?

165. Is the origin of the requirement clearly stated?

166. Are all functions required by the customer included?

167. What are current process problems?

168. What can tools do for us?

169. How do you know when a Requirement is accurate enough?

2.5 Requirements Traceability Matrix: Data Center Networking

170. How do you manage scope?

171. Will you use a Requirements Traceability Matrix?

172. Why do you manage scope?

173. What is the WBS?

174. What are the chronologies, contingencies, consequences, criteria?

175. Is there a requirements traceability process in place?

176. What percentage of Data Center Networking projects are producing traceability matrices between requirements and other work products?

177. Do you have a clear understanding of all subcontracts in place?

178. Describe the process for approving requirements so they can be added to the traceability matrix and Data Center Networking project work can be performed. Will the Data Center Networking project requirements become approved in writing?

179. How small is small enough?

180. How will it affect the stakeholders personally in

career?

181. Why use a WBS?

2.6 Project Scope Statement: Data Center Networking

182. Is an issue management process documented and filed?

183. What are the defined meeting materials?

184. Is the Data Center Networking project manager qualified and experienced in Data Center Networking project management?

185. Were key Data Center Networking project stakeholders brought into the Data Center Networking project Plan?

186. What is the product of this Data Center Networking project?

187. Has the Data Center Networking project scope statement been reviewed as part of the baseline process?

188. Change management vs. change leadership - what is the difference?

189. Is there an information system for the Data Center Networking project?

190. Are there completion/verification criteria defined for each task producing an output?

191. Is the Data Center Networking project

organization documented and on file?

192. Is the change control process documented and on file?

193. Elements of scope management that deal with concept development ?

194. Will statistics related to QA be collected, trends analyzed, and problems raised as issues?

195. Will the risk plan be updated on a regular and frequent basis?

196. Have you been able to easily identify success criteria and create objective measurements for each of the Data Center Networking project scopes goal statements?

197. Will the qa related information be reported regularly as part of the status reporting mechanisms?

198. Will all Data Center Networking project issues be unconditionally tracked through the issue resolution process?

199. What are the major deliverables of the Data Center Networking project?

2.7 Assumption and Constraint Log: Data Center Networking

200. What do you audit?

201. Diagrams and tables are included to account for complex concepts and increase overall readability?

202. Does a specific action and/or state that is known to violate security policy occur?

203. Have Data Center Networking project management standards and procedures been established and documented?

204. Are there processes in place to ensure that all the terms and code concepts have been documented consistently?

205. What weaknesses do you have?

206. Has the approach and development strategy of the Data Center Networking project been defined, documented and accepted by the appropriate stakeholders?

207. Do you know what your customers expectations are regarding this process?

208. What does an audit system look like?

209. Have all involved stakeholders and work groups committed to the Data Center Networking project?

210. Is there documentation of system capability requirements, data requirements, environment requirements, security requirements, and computer and hardware requirements?

211. How can you prevent/fix violations?

212. Should factors be unpredictable over time?

213. If appropriate, is the deliverable content consistent with current Data Center Networking project documents and in compliance with the Document Management Plan?

214. Is the definition of the Data Center Networking project scope clear; what needs to be accomplished?

215. Are there cosmetic errors that hinder readability and comprehension?

216. Are requirements management tracking tools and procedures in place?

217. Have all stakeholders been identified?

218. Are processes for release management of new development from coding and unit testing, to integration testing, to training, and production defined and followed?

219. Does the document/deliverable meet all requirements (for example, statement of work) specific to this deliverable?

2.8 Work Breakdown Structure: Data Center Networking

220. How will you and your Data Center Networking project team define the Data Center Networking projects scope and work breakdown structure?

221. Why is it useful?

222. What has to be done?

223. Is the work breakdown structure (wbs) defined and is the scope of the Data Center Networking project clear with assigned deliverable owners?

224. How many levels?

225. When does it have to be done?

226. Can you make it?

227. What is the probability of completing the Data Center Networking project in less that xx days?

228. Why would you develop a Work Breakdown Structure?

229. Where does it take place?

230. How big is a work-package?

231. How much detail?

232. Is it still viable?

233. What is the probability that the Data Center Networking project duration will exceed xx weeks?

234. Who has to do it?

235. When would you develop a Work Breakdown Structure?

236. When do you stop?

237. How far down?

2.9 WBS Dictionary: Data Center Networking

238. Are overhead budgets and costs being handled according to the disclosure statement when applicable, or otherwise properly classified (for example, engineering overhead, IR&D)?

239. Does the cost accumulation system provide for summarization of indirect costs from the point of allocation to the contract total?

240. Are estimates of costs at completion utilized in determining contract funding requirements and reporting them?

241. Does the contractors system provide for accurate cost accumulation and assignment to control accounts in a manner consistent with the budgets using recognized acceptable costing techniques?

242. Identify potential or actual budget-based and time-based schedule variances?

243. Are data elements (BCWS, BCWP, and ACWP) progressively summarized from the detail level to the contract level through the CWBS?

244. Do the lines of authority for incurring indirect costs correspond to the lines of responsibility for management control of the same components of costs?

245. Is the work done on a work package level as described in the WBS dictionary?

246. Does the scheduling system provide for the identification of work progress against technical and other milestones, and also provide for forecasts of completion dates of scheduled work?

247. Are detailed work packages planned as far in advance as practicable?

248. How detailed should a Data Center Networking project get?

249. Is the entire contract planned in time-phased control accounts to the extent practicable?

250. Are internal budgets for authorized, and not priced changes based on the contractors resource plan for accomplishing the work?

251. Are estimates developed by Data Center Networking project personnel coordinated with the already stated responsible for overall management to determine whether required resources will be available according to revised planning?

252. Do work packages reflect the actual way in which the work will be done and are they meaningful products or management-oriented subdivisions of a higher level element of work?

253. Contemplated overhead expenditure for each period based on the best information currently available?

254. Changes in the direct base to which overhead costs are allocated?

255. Should you include sub-activities?

2.10 Schedule Management Plan: Data Center Networking

256. Are the quality tools and methods identified in the Quality Plan appropriate to the Data Center Networking project?

257. Who is responsible for estimating the activity resources?

258. Are the activity durations realistic and at an appropriate level of detail for effective management?

259. Have Data Center Networking project success criteria been defined?

260. Are the people assigned to the Data Center Networking project sufficiently qualified?

261. Has the ims been resource-loaded and are assigned resources reasonable and available?

262. Do all stakeholders know how to access this repository and where to find the Data Center Networking project documentation?

263. Is there a formal set of procedures supporting Issues Management?

264. How are Data Center Networking projects different from operations?

265. Will the tools selected accomplish the scheduling

needs?

266. Is the schedule feasible and at what cost?

267. Is documentation created for communication with the suppliers and Vendors?

268. Has a sponsor been identified?

269. What tools and techniques will be used to estimate activity resources?

270. What will be the format of the schedule model?

271. Are Data Center Networking project leaders committed to this Data Center Networking project full time?

272. Are meeting objectives identified for each meeting?

2.11 Activity List: Data Center Networking

273. What went well?

274. What is the LF and LS for each activity?

275. In what sequence?

276. Who will perform the work?

277. For other activities, how much delay can be tolerated?

278. How difficult will it be to do specific activities on this Data Center Networking project?

279. What is the probability the Data Center Networking project can be completed in xx weeks?

280. Is there anything planned that does not need to be here?

281. How should ongoing costs be monitored to try to keep the Data Center Networking project within budget?

282. How do you determine the late start (LS) for each activity?

283. What are the critical bottleneck activities?

284. Where will it be performed?

285. How detailed should a Data Center Networking project get?

286. When do the individual activities need to start and finish?

287. Can you determine the activity that must finish, before this activity can start?

288. What is the total time required to complete the Data Center Networking project if no delays occur?

2.12 Activity Attributes: Data Center Networking

289. Can more resources be added?

290. Are the required resources available?

291. How do you manage time?

292. How difficult will it be to complete specific activities on this Data Center Networking project?

293. Has management defined a definite timeframe for the turnaround or Data Center Networking project window?

294. Which method produces the more accurate cost assignment?

295. Is there a trend during the year?

296. Are the required resources available or need to be acquired?

297. Does your organization of the data change its meaning?

298. Where else does it apply?

299. What is the general pattern here?

300. What is your organizations history in doing similar activities?

301. Time for overtime?

302. Would you consider either of corresponding activities an outlier?

303. How many resources do you need to complete the work scope within a limit of X number of days?

304. Do you feel very comfortable with your prediction?

305. Were there other ways you could have organized the data to achieve similar results?

306. How many days do you need to complete the work scope with a limit of X number of resources?

2.13 Milestone List: Data Center Networking

307. Environmental effects?

308. How will the milestone be verified?

309. Describe the industry you are in and the market growth opportunities. What is the market for your technology, product or service?

310. What specific improvements did you make to the Data Center Networking project proposal since the previous time?

311. Level of the Innovation?

312. How soon can the activity finish?

313. Obstacles faced?

314. Sustaining internal capabilities?

315. Do you foresee any technical risks or developmental challenges?

316. Reliability of data, plan predictability?

317. What has been done so far?

318. How difficult will it be to do specific activities on this Data Center Networking project?

319. Insurmountable weaknesses?

320. What is the market for your technology, product or service?

321. How late can each activity be finished and started?

322. What would happen if a delivery of material was one week late?

323. Timescales, deadlines and pressures?

324. Loss of key staff?

325. Describe your organizations strengths and core competencies. What factors will make your organization succeed?

2.14 Network Diagram: Data Center Networking

326. Planning: who, how long, what to do?

327. What must be completed before an activity can be started?

328. Can you calculate the confidence level?

329. What are the Key Success Factors?

330. What activity must be completed immediately before this activity can start?

331. Review the logical flow of the network diagram. Take a look at which activities you have first and then sequence the activities. Do they make sense?

332. What job or jobs follow it?

333. Will crashing x weeks return more in benefits than it costs?

334. What are the Major Administrative Issues?

335. Why must you schedule milestones, such as reviews, throughout the Data Center Networking project?

336. How difficult will it be to do specific activities on this Data Center Networking project?

337. What is the probability of completing the Data Center Networking project in less that xx days?

338. If the Data Center Networking project network diagram cannot change and you have extra personnel resources, what is the BEST thing to do?

339. What is the completion time?

340. What can be done concurrently?

341. What controls the start and finish of a job?

342. If a current contract exists, can you provide the vendor name, contract start, and contract expiration date?

2.15 Activity Resource Requirements: Data Center Networking

343. Do you use tools like decomposition and rolling-wave planning to produce the activity list and other outputs?

344. Anything else?

345. What is the Work Plan Standard?

346. Which logical relationship does the PDM use most often?

347. Organizational Applicability?

348. Why do you do that?

349. How many signatures do you require on a check and does this match what is in your policy and procedures?

350. What are constraints that you might find during the Human Resource Planning process?

351. How do you handle petty cash?

352. Are there unresolved issues that need to be addressed?

353. Other support in specific areas?

354. When does monitoring begin?

2.16 Resource Breakdown Structure: Data Center Networking

355. What is the primary purpose of the human resource plan?

356. Who will use the system?

357. Which resources should be in the resource pool?

358. Goals for the Data Center Networking project. What is each stakeholders desired outcome for the Data Center Networking project?

359. What defines a successful Data Center Networking project?

360. Is predictive resource analysis being done?

361. How should the information be delivered?

362. Who is allowed to see what data about which resources?

363. Who delivers the information?

364. What can you do to improve productivity?

365. What is the number one predictor of a groups productivity?

366. What is Data Center Networking project communication management?

367. Who needs what information?

368. Who will be used as a Data Center Networking project team member?

369. What defines a successful Data Center Networking project?

370. How can this help you with team building?

2.17 Activity Duration Estimates: Data Center Networking

371. If you plan to take the PMP exam soon, what should you do to prepare?

372. Do you think many other organizations could apply this methodology, or does each organization need to create its own methodology?

373. Why do you think schedule issues often cause the most conflicts on Data Center Networking projects?

374. Will it help in finding or retaining employees?

375. Are Data Center Networking project results verified and Data Center Networking project documents archived?

376. Consider the changes in the job market for information technology workers. How does the job market and current state of the economy affect human resource management?

377. How do functionality, system outputs, performance, reliability, and maintainability requirements affect quality planning?

378. Is risk identification completed regularly throughout the Data Center Networking project?

379. Does the case present a realistic scenario?

380. Will additional funds be needed for hardware or software?

381. How difficult will it be to complete specific activities on this Data Center Networking project?

382. Does a process exist for approving or rejecting changes?

383. Are reward and recognition systems defined to promote or reinforce desired behavior?

384. Would you rate yourself as being risk-averse, risk-neutral, or risk-seeking?

385. Do stakeholders follow a procedure for formally accepting the Data Center Networking project scope?

386. Briefly describe some key events in the history of Data Center Networking project management. What Data Center Networking project was the first to use modern Data Center Networking project management?

387. Is the Data Center Networking project performing better or worse than planned?

388. What type of contract was used and why?

389. After changes are approved are Data Center Networking project documents updated and distributed?

390. What do you think the real problem was in this case?

2.18 Duration Estimating Worksheet: Data Center Networking

391. Why estimate time and cost?

392. Does the Data Center Networking project provide innovative ways for stakeholders to overcome obstacles or deliver better outcomes?

393. Is the Data Center Networking project responsive to community need?

394. When does your organization expect to be able to complete it?

395. What questions do you have?

396. Value pocket identification & quantification what are value pockets?

397. Will the Data Center Networking project collaborate with the local community and leverage resources?

398. What is next?

399. Define the work as completely as possible. What work will be included in the Data Center Networking project?

400. What is the total time required to complete the Data Center Networking project if no delays occur?

401. How should ongoing costs be monitored to try to keep the Data Center Networking project within budget?

402. What is your role?

403. What info is needed?

404. What is an Average Data Center Networking project?

405. Is a construction detail attached (to aid in explanation)?

406. What utility impacts are there?

407. Do any colleagues have experience with your organization and/or RFPs?

408. Why estimate costs?

409. What work will be included in the Data Center Networking project?

2.19 Project Schedule: Data Center Networking

410. Is Data Center Networking project work proceeding in accordance with the original Data Center Networking project schedule?

411. How does a Data Center Networking project get to be a year late ?

412. How do you manage Data Center Networking project Risk?

413. How can slack be negative?

414. Why time management?

415. How do you know that youhave done this right?

416. Are all remaining durations correct?

417. How closely did the initial Data Center Networking project Schedule compare with the actual schedule?

418. How can you fix it?

419. Should you have a test for each code module?

420. If you can not fix it, how do you do it differently?

421. Are key risk mitigation strategies added to the Data Center Networking project schedule?

422. How can you shorten the schedule?

423. Why is this particularly bad?

424. Is the structure for tracking the Data Center Networking project schedule well defined and assigned to a specific individual?

425. Are quality inspections and review activities listed in the Data Center Networking project schedule(s)?

426. Is the Data Center Networking project schedule available for all Data Center Networking project team members to review?

427. Are there activities that came from a template or previous Data Center Networking project that are not applicable on this phase of this Data Center Networking project?

428. Why or why not?

2.20 Cost Management Plan: Data Center Networking

429. Similar Data Center Networking projects?

430. Are target dates established for each milestone deliverable?

431. Is there general agreement & acceptance of the current status and progress of the Data Center Networking project?

432. Are the Data Center Networking project team members located locally to the users/stakeholders?

433. Have all unresolved risks been documented?

434. Data Center Networking project Objectives?

435. Owner, contractor, and subcontractors?

436. Has a structured approach been used to break work effort into manageable components (WBS)?

437. Were Data Center Networking project team members involved in the development of activity & task decomposition?

438. Progress measurement and control – How will the Data Center Networking project measure and control progress?

439. Vac -variance at completion, how much over/

under budget do you expect to be?

440. Responsibilities – what is the split of responsibilities between the owner and contractors?

441. How does the proposed individual meet each requirement?

442. Have the procedures for identifying budget variances been followed?

443. Is there anything unique in this Data Center Networking projects scope statement that will affect resources?

444. Are post milestone Data Center Networking project reviews (PMPR) conducted with your organization at least once a year?

2.21 Activity Cost Estimates: Data Center Networking

445. Specific - is the objective clear in terms of what, how, when, and where the situation will be changed?

446. Will you use any tools, such as Data Center Networking project management software, to assist in capturing Earned Value metrics?

447. Were you satisfied with the work?

448. What is included in indirect cost being allocated?

449. Certification of actual expenditures?

450. Does the activity serve a common type of customer?

451. What areas does the group agree are the biggest success on the Data Center Networking project?

452. Were escalated issues resolved promptly?

453. Estimated cost?

454. Why do you manage cost?

455. What areas were overlooked on this Data Center Networking project?

456. What makes a good expected result statement?

457. What is the Data Center Networking projects sustainability strategy that will ensure Data Center Networking project results will endure or be sustained?

458. What is the activity inventory?

459. Padding is bad and contingencies are good. what is the difference?

460. When do you enter into PPM?

461. Were the costs or charges reasonable?

462. How do you fund change orders?

2.22 Cost Estimating Worksheet: Data Center Networking

463. Identify the timeframe necessary to monitor progress and collect data to determine how the selected measure has changed?

464. What happens to any remaining funds not used?

465. What is the estimated labor cost today based upon this information?

466. What will others want?

467. Is it feasible to establish a control group arrangement?

468. How will the results be shared and to whom?

469. Who is best positioned to know and assist in identifying corresponding factors?

470. What costs are to be estimated?

471. Can a trend be established from historical performance data on the selected measure and are the criteria for using trend analysis or forecasting methods met?

472. Will the Data Center Networking project collaborate with the local community and leverage resources?

473. What additional Data Center Networking project(s) could be initiated as a result of this Data Center Networking project?

474. What is the purpose of estimating?

475. Ask: are others positioned to know, are others credible, and will others cooperate?

476. Is the Data Center Networking project responsive to community need?

477. What can be included?

478. Does the Data Center Networking project provide innovative ways for stakeholders to overcome obstacles or deliver better outcomes?

2.23 Cost Baseline: Data Center Networking

479. How will cost estimates be used?

480. Are there contingencies or conditions related to the acceptance?

481. For what purpose ?

482. Should a more thorough impact analysis be conducted?

483. What is your organizations history in doing similar tasks?

484. Is there anything unique in this Data Center Networking projects scope statement that will affect resources?

485. On budget?

486. How long are you willing to wait before you find out were late?

487. Has the actual cost of the Data Center Networking project (or Data Center Networking project phase) been tallied and compared to the approved budget?

488. Is there anything you need from upper management in order to be successful?

489. Have all approved changes to the cost baseline been identified and impact on the Data Center Networking project documented?

490. Where do changes come from?

491. Have all approved changes to the Data Center Networking project requirement been identified and impact on the performance, cost, and schedule baselines documented?

492. Have the actual milestone completion dates been compared to the approved schedule?

493. What would the life cycle costs be?

494. Have all the product or service deliverables been accepted by the customer?

495. What threats might prevent you from getting there?

496. What do you want to measure ?

497. Are you asking management for something as a result of this update?

2.24 Quality Management Plan: Data Center Networking

498. What are you trying to accomplish?

499. How do you prioritize?

500. What data do you gather/use/compile?

501. Sampling part of task?

502. Who is responsible for writing the qapp?

503. Documented results available?

504. How do senior leaders create an environment that encourages learning and innovation?

505. Are formal code reviews conducted?

506. Is this a Requirement?

507. What key performance indicators does your organization use to measure, manage, and improve key processes?

508. Diagrams and tables to account for complex concepts and increase overall readability?

509. Are you following the quality standards?

510. What changes can you make that will result in improvement?

511. Methodology followed?

512. List your organizations customer contact standards that employees are expected to maintain. How are corresponding standards measured?

513. How does your organization maintain a safe and healthy work environment?

514. Does the Data Center Networking project have a formal Data Center Networking project Plan?

515. How do senior leaders create and communicate values and performance expectations?

516. Who gets results of work?

2.25 Quality Metrics: Data Center Networking

517. How effective are your security tests?

518. Has trace of defects been initiated?

519. What if the biggest risk to your business were the already stated people who do not complain?

520. Does risk analysis documentation meet standards?

521. What metrics are important and most beneficial to measure?

522. Is a risk containment plan in place?

523. What makes a visualization memorable?

524. When is the security analysis testing complete?

525. What are your organizations expectations for its quality Data Center Networking project?

526. Were quality attributes reported?

527. How do you know if everyone is trying to improve the right things?

528. Are quality metrics defined?

529. Who notifies stakeholders of normal and

abnormal results?

530. Can you correlate your quality metrics to profitability?

531. Do the operators focus on determining; is there anything you need to worry about?

532. Where is quality now?

533. What level of statistical confidence do you use?

534. What is the benchmark?

2.26 Process Improvement Plan: Data Center Networking

535. Have the supporting tools been developed or acquired?

536. Are you making progress on the improvement framework?

537. Has a process guide to collect the data been developed?

538. Why do you want to achieve the goal?

539. Does your process ensure quality?

540. Where are you now?

541. What is quality and how will you ensure it?

542. Everyone agrees on what process improvement is, right?

543. Are you making progress on your improvement plan?

544. Are there forms and procedures to collect and record the data?

545. The motive is determined by asking, Why do you want to achieve this goal?

546. Where do you want to be?

547. Have the frequency of collection and the points in the process where measurements will be made been determined?

548. Management commitment at all levels?

549. What personnel are the coaches for your initiative?

550. Modeling current processes is great, and will you ever see a return on that investment?

551. What lessons have you learned so far?

2.27 Responsibility Assignment Matrix: Data Center Networking

552. Are all elements of indirect expense identified to overhead cost budgets of Data Center Networking projections?

553. Past experience – the person or the group worked at something similar in the past?

554. Are overhead cost budgets established for each organization which has authority to incur overhead costs?

555. When performing is split among two or more roles, is the work clearly defined so that the efforts are coordinated and the communication is clear?

556. What cost control tool do many experts say is crucial to Data Center Networking project management?

557. Does a missing responsibility indicate that the current Data Center Networking project is not yet fully understood?

558. The anticipated business volume?

559. Is accountability placed at the lowest-possible level within the Data Center Networking project so that decisions can be made at that level?

560. Why cost benefit analysis?

561. What expertise is not available in your department?

562. Do others have the time to dedicate to your Data Center Networking project?

563. Budgeted cost for work scheduled?

564. Performance to date and material commitment?

565. Evaluate the impact of schedule changes, work around, etc?

566. Are there any drawbacks to using a responsibility assignment matrix?

567. The staff characteristics – is the group or the person capable to work together as a team?

568. Data Center Networking projected economic escalation?

569. Not any rs, as, or cs: if an identified role is only informed, should others be eliminated from the matrix?

570. Are indirect costs charged to the appropriate indirect pools and incurring organization?

571. Who is the Data Center Networking project Manager?

2.28 Roles and Responsibilities: Data Center Networking

572. Who is involved?

573. Key conclusions and recommendations: Are conclusions and recommendations relevant and acceptable?

574. Is the data complete?

575. Are Data Center Networking project team roles and responsibilities identified and documented?

576. Who is responsible for implementation activities and where will the functions, roles and responsibilities be defined?

577. What specific behaviors did you observe?

578. Have you ever been a part of this team?

579. What areas of supervision are challenging for you?

580. What is working well?

581. Concern: where are you limited or have no authority, where you can not influence?

582. Are your budgets supportive of a culture of quality data?

583. How is your work-life balance?

584. Do the values and practices inherent in the culture of your organization foster or hinder the process?

585. Be specific; avoid generalities. Thank you and great work alone are insufficient. What exactly do you appreciate and why?

586. Accountabilities: what are the roles and responsibilities of individual team members?

587. Attainable / achievable: the goal is attainable; can you actually accomplish the goal?

588. Once the responsibilities are defined for the Data Center Networking project, have the deliverables, roles and responsibilities been clearly communicated to every participant?

589. Is feedback clearly communicated and non-judgmental?

590. Was the expectation clearly communicated?

591. Who: who is involved?

2.29 Human Resource Management Plan: Data Center Networking

592. What areas does the group agree are the biggest success on the Data Center Networking project?

593. Are estimating assumptions and constraints captured?

594. Do you have the reasons why the changes to your organizational systems and capabilities are required?

595. Is a stakeholder management plan in place that covers topics?

596. How to convince employees that this is a necessary process?

597. Was your organizations estimating methodology being used and followed?

598. Are written status reports provided on a designated frequent basis?

599. Do Data Center Networking project teams & team members report on status / activities / progress?

600. Is current scope of the Data Center Networking project substantially different than that originally defined?

601. Has a quality assurance plan been developed for

the Data Center Networking project?

602. Are all vendor contracts closed out?

603. Is stakeholder involvement adequate?

604. How well does your organization communicate?

605. Are procurement deliverables arriving on time and to specification?

606. Is there a Quality Management Plan?

607. Are adequate resources provided for the quality assurance function?

608. Are the results of quality assurance reviews provided to affected groups & individuals?

609. Are status reports received per the Data Center Networking project Plan?

610. Is Data Center Networking project work proceeding in accordance with the original Data Center Networking project schedule?

611. Is an industry recognized support tool(s) being used for Data Center Networking project scheduling & tracking?

2.30 Communications Management Plan: Data Center Networking

612. What data is going to be required?

613. What is the political influence?

614. Who are the members of the governing body?

615. What does the stakeholder need from the team?

616. Are others part of the communications management plan?

617. Who is responsible?

618. What help do you and your team need from the stakeholder?

619. Who did you turn to if you had questions?

620. What is the stakeholders level of authority?

621. Are the stakeholders getting the information others need, are others consulted, are concerns addressed?

622. Will messages be directly related to the release strategy or phases of the Data Center Networking project?

623. Who to learn from?

624. Can you think of other people who might have concerns or interests?

625. Are there too many who have an interest in some aspect of your work?

626. Timing: when do the effects of the communication take place?

627. Who to share with?

628. What are the interrelationships?

629. Is there an important stakeholder who is actively opposed and will not receive messages?

630. How often do you engage with stakeholders?

631. How is this initiative related to other portfolios, programs, or Data Center Networking projects?

2.31 Risk Management Plan: Data Center Networking

632. Are tool mentors available?

633. Are certain activities taking a long time to complete?

634. What can you do to minimize the impact if it does?

635. Financial risk: can your organization afford to undertake the Data Center Networking project?

636. What are it-specific requirements?

637. Are staff committed for the duration of the product?

638. Is the customer willing to commit significant time to the requirements gathering process?

639. Degree of confidence in estimated size estimate?

640. Does the software engineering team have the right mix of skills?

641. Do the people have the right combinations of skills?

642. Do the requirements require the creation of components that are unlike anything your organization has previously built?

643. Which is an input to the risk management process?

644. Was an original risk assessment/risk management plan completed?

645. Do you train all developers in the process?

646. Why is product liability a serious issue?

647. Where are you confronted with risks during the business phases?

648. Are the reports useful and easy to read?

649. Are team members trained in the use of the tools?

2.32 Risk Register: Data Center Networking

650. Are there any knock-on effects/impact on any of the other areas?

651. Have other controls and solutions been implemented in other services which could be applied as an alternative to additional funding?

652. Cost/benefit – how much will the proposed mitigations cost and how does this cost compare with the potential cost of the risk event/situation should it occur?

653. What can be done about it?

654. What is a Risk?

655. What should you do now?

656. Financial risk -can your organization afford to undertake the Data Center Networking project?

657. How is a Community Risk Register created?

658. How are risks identified?

659. Contingency actions - planned actions to reduce the immediate seriousness of the risk when it does occur. What should you do when?

660. Budget and schedule: what are the estimated

costs and schedules for performing risk-related activities?

661. Is further information required before making a decision?

662. What could prevent you delivering on the strategic program objectives and what is being done to mitigate corresponding issues?

663. Amongst the action plans and recommendations that you have to introduce are there some that could stop or delay the overall program?

664. User involvement: do you have the right users?

665. Risk categories: what are the main categories of risks that should be addressed on this Data Center Networking project?

666. Severity Prediction?

667. What would the impact to the Data Center Networking project objectives be should the risk arise?

668. Are implemented controls working as others should?

2.33 Probability and Impact Assessment: Data Center Networking

669. How would you suggest monitoring for risk transition indicators?

670. Will new information become available during the Data Center Networking project?

671. Have you worked with the customer in the past?

672. Is it necessary to deeply assess all Data Center Networking project risks?

673. Are requirements fully understood by the software engineering team and customers?

674. When and how will the recent breakthroughs in basic research lead to commercial products?

675. Are staff committed for the duration of the Data Center Networking project?

676. Sensitivity analysis -which risks will have the most impact on the Data Center Networking project?

677. Who will be responsible for a slippage?

678. What can you do about it?

679. What action do you usually take against risks?

680. What are the probabilities of chosen technologies

being suitable for local conditions?

681. Is the delay in one subData Center Networking project going to affect another?

682. How would you assess the risk management process in the Data Center Networking project?

683. How will economic events and trends likely affect the Data Center Networking project?

684. What are the likely future requirements?

685. What significant shift will occur in governmental policies, laws, and regulations pertaining to specific industries?

686. How well is the risk understood?

687. How are the local factors going to affect the absorption?

688. How is risk handled within this Data Center Networking project organization?

2.34 Probability and Impact Matrix: Data Center Networking

689. What are data sources?

690. Do you have specific methods that you use for each phase of the process?

691. How realistic is the timing of introduction?

692. Mandated delivery date?

693. What can go wrong?

694. Have staff received necessary training?

695. Who are the owners?

696. Are there new risks that mitigation strategies might introduce?

697. During Data Center Networking project executing, a team member identifies a risk that is not in the risk register. What should you do?

698. Is the technology to be built new to your organization?

699. Workarounds are determined during which step of risk management?

700. Is Data Center Networking project scope stable?

701. What things might go wrong?

702. Mandated specific features?

703. Prioritized components/features?

704. Are enough people available?

705. What are the current or emerging trends of culture?

706. How carefully have the potential competitors been identified?

2.35 Risk Data Sheet: Data Center Networking

707. Has the most cost-effective solution been chosen?

708. What will be the consequences if it happens?

709. Will revised controls lead to tolerable risk levels?

710. What are the main opportunities available to you that you should grab while you can?

711. What is the environment within which you operate (social trends, economic, community values, broad based participation, national directions etc.)?

712. What is the chance that it will happen?

713. What do people affected think about the need for, and practicality of preventive measures?

714. What can happen?

715. How reliable is the data source?

716. Potential for recurrence?

717. Is the data sufficiently specified in terms of the type of failure being analyzed, and its frequency or probability?

718. Has a sensitivity analysis been carried out?

719. What actions can be taken to eliminate or remove risk?

720. What are the main threats to your existence?

721. What are you trying to achieve (Objectives)?

722. What can you do?

723. What is the likelihood of it happening?

724. Do effective diagnostic tests exist?

725. During work activities could hazards exist?

726. What were the Causes that contributed?

2.36 Procurement Management Plan: Data Center Networking

727. Is there a set of procedures to capture, analyze and act on quality metrics?

728. If independent estimates will be needed as evaluation criteria, who will prepare them and when?

729. Have stakeholder accountabilities & responsibilities been clearly defined?

730. Does the Data Center Networking project team have the right skills?

731. Were Data Center Networking project team members involved in the development of activity & task decomposition?

732. Is the Data Center Networking project schedule available for all Data Center Networking project team members to review?

733. How will multiple providers be managed?

734. Are vendor invoices audited for accuracy before payment?

735. Pareto diagrams, statistical sampling, flow charting or trend analysis used quality monitoring?

736. Are issues raised, assessed, actioned, and resolved in a timely and efficient manner?

737. Are parking lot items captured?

738. Is there a procurement management plan in place?

739. Are actuals compared against estimates to analyze and correct variances?

740. Is a payment system in place with proper reviews and approvals?

741. Has a resource management plan been created?

2.37 Source Selection Criteria: Data Center Networking

742. What is the effect of the debriefing schedule on potential protests?

743. Are evaluators ready to begin this task?

744. What aspects should the contracting officer brief the Data Center Networking project on prior to evaluation of proposals?

745. How much weight should be placed on past performance information?

746. What does an evaluation address and what does a sample resemble?

747. How will you decide an evaluators write up is sufficient?

748. How organization are proposed quotes/prices?

749. What should be the contracting officers strategy?

750. What information is to be provided and when should it be provided?

751. What can not be disclosed?

752. What are the guidelines regarding award without considerations?

753. Who is entitled to a debriefing?

754. What is price analysis and when should it be performed?

755. How should oral presentations be prepared for?

756. How can business terms and conditions be improved to yield more effective price competition?

757. Are there any specific considerations that precludes offers from being selected as the awardee?

758. Do you want to have them collaborate at subfactor level?

759. Do you prepare an independent cost estimate?

760. Is a letter of commitment from each proposed team member and key subcontractor included?

761. How do you ensure an integrated assessment of proposals?

2.38 Stakeholder Management Plan: Data Center Networking

762. Will Data Center Networking project success require up to date information at a moments notice?

763. Does all Data Center Networking project documentation reside in a common repository for easy access?

764. Has the budget been baselined?

765. Have external dependencies been captured in the schedule?

766. What is the drawback in using qualitative Data Center Networking project selection techniques?

767. When would you develop a Data Center Networking project Execution Plan?

768. What are the advantages and disadvantages of using external contracted resources?

769. Is the process working, and are people executing in compliance of the process?

770. Have the key functions and capabilities been defined and assigned to each release or iteration?

771. Are the appropriate IT resources adequate to meet planned commitments?

772. Have reserves been created to address risks?

773. Do you use diagrams and tables to account for complex concepts and increase overall readability?

774. Are software metrics formally captured, analyzed and used as a basis for other Data Center Networking project estimates?

775. Are there standards for code development?

776. Are best practices and metrics employed to identify issues, progress, performance, etc.?

777. Has the scope management document been updated and distributed to help prevent scope creep?

778. Are corrective actions and variances reported?

779. Why would you develop a Data Center Networking project Business Plan?

780. Who will perform the review(s)?

781. What guidelines or procedures currently exist that must be adhered to (eg departmental accounting procedures)?

2.39 Change Management Plan: Data Center Networking

782. Has the target training audience been identified and nominated?

783. Is there support for this application(s) and are the details available for distribution?

784. What are the specific target groups / audience that will be impacted by this change?

785. What work practices will be affected?

786. What are the major changes to processes?

787. What provokes organizational change?

788. Where will the funds come from?

789. Has the priority for this Data Center Networking project been set by the Business Unit Management Team?

790. What is the negative impact of communicating too soon or too late?

791. Who should be involved in developing a change management strategy?

792. What new roles are needed?

793. What are the specific target groups/audiences

that will be impacted by this change?

794. What does a resilient organization look like?

795. What is the most positive interpretation it can receive?

796. What would be an estimate of the total cost for the activities required to carry out the change initiative?

797. How prevalent is Resistance to Change?

798. How will you deal with anger about the restricting of communications due to confidentiality considerations?

799. Do you need a new organizational structure?

800. Who will do the training?

801. How far reaching in your organization is the change?

3.0 Executing Process Group: Data Center Networking

802. What are the main types of goods and services being outsourced?

803. What are the main processes included in Data Center Networking project quality management?

804. How will you avoid scope creep?

805. How do you prevent staff are just doing busywork to pass the time?

806. How is Data Center Networking project performance information created and distributed?

807. How could you control progress of your Data Center Networking project?

808. How can software assist in procuring goods and services?

809. How can software assist in Data Center Networking project communications?

810. Is the Data Center Networking project performing better or worse than planned?

811. Just how important is your work to the overall success of the Data Center Networking project?

812. Based on your Data Center Networking project

communication management plan, what worked well?

813. If action is called for, what form should it take?

814. Will new hardware or software be required for servers or client machines?

815. After how many days will the lease cost be the same as the purchase cost for the equipment?

816. What does it mean to take a systems view of a Data Center Networking project?

817. What areas were overlooked on this Data Center Networking project?

818. How do you control progress of your Data Center Networking project?

819. When is the appropriate time to bring the scorecard to Board meetings?

3.1 Team Member Status Report: Data Center Networking

820. Does your organization have the means (staff, money, contract, etc.) to produce or to acquire the product, good, or service?

821. Are the products of your organizations Data Center Networking projects meeting customers objectives?

822. When a teams productivity and success depend on collaboration and the efficient flow of information, what generally fails them?

823. How much risk is involved?

824. Will the staff do training or is that done by a third party?

825. Does the product, good, or service already exist within your organization?

826. How will resource planning be done?

827. How it is to be done?

828. Do you have an Enterprise Data Center Networking project Management Office (EPMO)?

829. How can you make it practical?

830. Is there evidence that staff is taking a more

professional approach toward management of your organizations Data Center Networking projects?

831. Are your organizations Data Center Networking projects more successful over time?

832. How does this product, good, or service meet the needs of the Data Center Networking project and your organization as a whole?

833. Does every department have to have a Data Center Networking project Manager on staff?

834. What is to be done?

835. Why is it to be done?

836. Are the attitudes of staff regarding Data Center Networking project work improving?

837. What specific interest groups do you have in place?

838. The problem with Reward & Recognition Programs is that the truly deserving people all too often get left out. How can you make it practical?

3.2 Change Request: Data Center Networking

839. Who is communicating the change?

840. How does your organization control changes before and after software is released to a customer?

841. Why do you want to have a change control system?

842. How are the measures for carrying out the change established?

843. What are the Impacts to your organization?

844. Why were your requested changes rejected or not made?

845. Since there are no change requests in your Data Center Networking project at this point, what must you have before you begin?

846. Have scm procedures for noting the change, recording it, and reporting it been followed?

847. Change request coordination ?

848. What are the requirements for urgent changes?

849. Why control change across the life cycle?

850. How is quality being addressed on the Data

Center Networking project?

851. What mechanism is used to appraise others of changes that are made?

852. How can you ensure that changes have been made properly?

853. Who is responsible for the implementation and monitoring of all measures?

854. Who is responsible to authorize changes?

855. What is the function of the change control committee?

856. How do team members communicate with each other?

857. What are the duties of the change control team?

858. How shall the implementation of changes be recorded?

3.3 Change Log: Data Center Networking

859. Is the change request open, closed or pending?

860. Is the submitted change a new change or a modification of a previously approved change?

861. When was the request submitted?

862. Is the change backward compatible without limitations?

863. Does the suggested change request represent a desired enhancement to the products functionality?

864. Does the suggested change request seem to represent a necessary enhancement to the product?

865. Is this a mandatory replacement?

866. How does this change affect scope?

867. Do the described changes impact on the integrity or security of the system?

868. How does this change affect the timeline of the schedule?

869. When was the request approved?

870. Is the requested change request a result of changes in other Data Center Networking project(s)?

871. Is the change request within Data Center Networking project scope?

872. Will the Data Center Networking project fail if the change request is not executed?

873. How does this relate to the standards developed for specific business processes?

874. Who initiated the change request?

3.4 Decision Log: Data Center Networking

875. How do you define success?

876. How does provision of information, both in terms of content and presentation, influence acceptance of alternative strategies?

877. Does anything need to be adjusted?

878. What is your overall strategy for quality control / quality assurance procedures?

879. Linked to original objective?

880. Is everything working as expected?

881. How does the use a Decision Support System influence the strategies/tactics or costs?

882. Who is the decisionmaker?

883. It becomes critical to track and periodically revisit both operational effectiveness; Are you noticing all that you need to, and are you interpreting what you see effectively?

884. Decision-making process; how will the team make decisions?

885. How do you know when you are achieving it?

886. What eDiscovery problem or issue did your organization set out to fix or make better?

887. How consolidated and comprehensive a story can you tell by capturing currently available incident data in a central location and through a log of key decisions during an incident?

888. What alternatives/risks were considered?

889. What are the cost implications?

890. Do strategies and tactics aimed at less than full control reduce the costs of management or simply shift the cost burden?

891. Behaviors; what are guidelines that the team has identified that will assist them with getting the most out of team meetings?

892. What is the line where eDiscovery ends and document review begins?

893. What is the average size of your matters in an applicable measurement?

894. Which variables make a critical difference?

3.5 Quality Audit: Data Center Networking

895. How does your organization know that its processes for managing severance are appropriately effective, constructive and fair?

896. Are adequate and conveniently located toilet facilities available for use by the employees?

897. Have the risks associated with the intentions been identified, analyzed and appropriate responses developed?

898. How does your organization know that it is effectively and constructively guiding staff through to timely completion of tasks?

899. Health and safety arrangements; stress management workshops. How does your organization know that it provides a safe and healthy environment?

900. How does your organization know that its relationship with its (past) staff is appropriately effective and constructive?

901. What are your supplier audits?

902. Does your organization have set of goals, objectives, strategies and targets that are clearly understood by the Board and staff?

903. How does your organization know that its system

for attending to the health and wellbeing of its staff is appropriately effective and constructive?

904. Are there appropriate means for intervening if necessary?

905. Does the suppliers quality system have a written procedure for corrective action when a defect occurs?

906. Are training programs documented?

907. Are people allowed to contribute ideas?

908. How does your organization know that its promotions system is appropriately effective, constructive and fair?

909. Are all staff empowered and encouraged to contribute to ongoing improvement efforts?

910. Are multiple statements on the same issue consistent with each other?

911. Is refuse and garbage adequately stored and disposed of with sufficient frequency to prevent contamination?

912. How does your organization know that its system for recruiting the best staff possible are appropriately effective and constructive?

913. Has a written procedure been established to identify devices during all stages of receipt, reconditioning, distribution and installation so that mix-ups are prevented?

914. How does your organization know that its staff are presenting original work, and properly acknowledging the work of others?

3.6 Team Directory: Data Center Networking

915. How will the team handle changes?

916. Is construction on schedule?

917. How does the team resolve conflicts and ensure tasks are completed?

918. Who will report Data Center Networking project status to all stakeholders?

919. Have you decided when to celebrate the Data Center Networking projects completion date?

920. Who is the Sponsor?

921. Who are your stakeholders (customers, sponsors, end users, team members)?

922. Who are the Team Members?

923. Days from the time the issue is identified?

924. Who should receive information (all stakeholders)?

925. Process decisions: do job conditions warrant additional actions to collect job information and document on-site activity?

926. Who will talk to the customer?

927. How and in what format should information be presented?

928. Do purchase specifications and configurations match requirements?

929. Process decisions: which organizational elements and which individuals will be assigned management functions?

930. Decisions: is the most suitable form of contract being used?

931. Why is the work necessary?

932. What needs to be communicated?

933. Where will the product be used and/or delivered or built when appropriate?

3.7 Team Operating Agreement: Data Center Networking

934. Seconds for members to respond?

935. What are the current caseload numbers in the unit?

936. Do you determine the meeting length and time of day?

937. To whom do you deliver your services?

938. Are leadership responsibilities shared among team members (versus a single leader)?

939. Are there influences outside the team that may affect performance, and if so, have you identified and addressed them?

940. Do you listen for voice tone and word choice to understand the meaning behind words?

941. Do you post any action items, due dates, and responsibilities on the team website?

942. Communication protocols: how will the team communicate?

943. How will you resolve conflict efficiently and respectfully?

944. How will you divide work equitably?

945. Has the appropriate access to relevant data and analysis capability been granted?

946. Resource allocation: how will individual team members account for time and expenses, and how will this be allocated in the team budget?

947. Are team roles clearly defined and accepted?

948. What is the anticipated procedure (recruitment, solicitation of volunteers, or assignment) for selecting team members?

949. Methodologies: how will key team processes be implemented, such as training, research, work deliverable production, review and approval processes, knowledge management, and meeting procedures?

950. Are there more than two native languages represented by your team?

951. Did you prepare participants for the next meeting?

952. How will group handle unplanned absences?

3.8 Team Performance Assessment: Data Center Networking

953. To what degree does the team possess adequate membership to achieve its ends?

954. Individual task proficiency and team process behavior: what is important for team functioning?

955. To what degree are corresponding categories of skills either actually or potentially represented across the membership?

956. Can familiarity breed backup?

957. To what degree will the approach capitalize on and enhance the skills of all team members in a manner that takes into consideration other demands on members of the team?

958. When a reviewer complains about method variance, what is the essence of the complaint?

959. If you have criticized someones work for method variance in your role as reviewer, what was the circumstance?

960. To what degree can team members vigorously define the teams purpose in considerations with others who are not part of the functioning team?

961. How do you keep key people outside the group informed about its accomplishments?

962. What makes opportunities more or less obvious?

963. To what degree can team members frequently and easily communicate with one another?

964. Effects of crew composition on crew performance: Does the whole equal the sum of its parts?

965. To what degree do members understand and articulate the same purpose without relying on ambiguous abstractions?

966. Social categorization and intergroup behaviour: Does minimal intergroup discrimination make social identity more positive?

967. To what degree do team members articulate the teams work approach?

968. To what degree will team members, individually and collectively, commit time to help themselves and others learn and develop skills?

969. How do you recognize and praise members for contributions?

970. If you have received criticism from reviewers that your work suffered from method variance, what was the circumstance?

971. To what degree are the goals realistic?

972. How do you encourage members to learn from each other?

3.9 Team Member Performance Assessment: Data Center Networking

973. How do you currently use the time that is available?

974. How is your organizations Strategic Management System tied to performance measurement?

975. What is the role of the Reviewer?

976. To what degree do all members feel responsible for all agreed-upon measures?

977. To what degree does the teams approach to its work allow for modification and improvement over time?

978. Is there reluctance to join a team?

979. To what degree can team members meet frequently enough to accomplish the teams ends?

980. What is the Business Management Oversight Process?

981. To what degree are the skill areas critical to team performance present?

982. To what degree will new and supplemental skills be introduced as the need is recognized?

983. To what degree can all members engage in open

and interactive considerations?

984. What changes do you need to make to align practices with beliefs?

985. Does the rater (supervisor) have to wait for the interim or final performance assessment review to tell an employee that the employees performance is unsatisfactory?

986. What qualities does a successful Team leader possess?

987. To what degree can the team measure progress against specific goals?

988. What are the basic principles and objectives of performance measurement and assessment?

989. Who they are?

990. What stakeholders must be involved in the development and oversight of the performance plan?

991. What are top priorities?

3.10 Issue Log: Data Center Networking

992. Are the stakeholders getting the information they need, are they consulted, are concerns addressed?

993. Do you have members of your team responsible for certain stakeholders?

994. Who have you worked with in past, similar initiatives?

995. How do you manage human resources?

996. Who needs to know and how much?

997. Who reported the issue?

998. What are the typical contents?

999. Who is involved as you identify stakeholders?

1000. Why do you manage communications?

1001. What approaches do you use?

1002. Which stakeholders can influence others?

1003. Why multiple evaluators?

1004. In your work, how much time is spent on stakeholder identification?

1005. What effort will a change need?

1006. What approaches to you feel are the best ones to use?

1007. What is a Stakeholder?

4.0 Monitoring and Controlling Process Group: Data Center Networking

1008. What good practices or successful experiences or transferable examples have been identified?

1009. What were things that you did very well and want to do the same again on the next Data Center Networking project?

1010. How can you monitor progress?

1011. What is the timeline?

1012. Did the Data Center Networking project team have the right skills?

1013. How is agile program management done?

1014. Are the necessary foundations in place to ensure the sustainability of the results of the programme?

1015. How is agile Data Center Networking project management done?

1016. Is it what was agreed upon?

1017. How will staff learn how to use the deliverables?

1018. What is the timeline for the Data Center Networking project?

1019. How is agile portfolio management done?

1020. Is progress on outcomes due to your program?

1021. Is there sufficient funding available for this?

1022. If a risk event occurs, what will you do?

1023. Do the partners have sufficient financial capacity to keep up the benefits produced by the programme?

1024. Where is the Risk in the Data Center Networking project?

1025. What departments are involved in its daily operation?

4.1 Project Performance Report: Data Center Networking

1026. To what degree are the demands of the task compatible with and converge with the mission and functions of the formal organization?

1027. To what degree does the task meet individual needs?

1028. How is the data used?

1029. To what degree can the team ensure that all members are individually and jointly accountable for the teams purpose, goals, approach, and work-products?

1030. To what degree are the tasks requirements reflected in the flow and storage of information?

1031. To what degree do the goals specify concrete team work products?

1032. To what degree does the teams work approach provide opportunity for members to engage in fact-based problem solving?

1033. To what degree does the funding match the requirement?

1034. To what degree will each member have the opportunity to advance his or her professional skills in all three of the above categories while contributing to the accomplishment of the teams purpose and goals?

1035. What is the PRS?

1036. To what degree does the teams purpose constitute a broader, deeper aspiration than just accomplishing short-term goals?

1037. To what degree does the teams purpose contain themes that are particularly meaningful and memorable?

1038. To what degree does the formal organization make use of individual resources and meet individual needs?

1039. To what degree do members articulate the goals beyond the team membership?

1040. To what degree does the information network communicate information relevant to the task?

1041. To what degree do team members understand one anothers roles and skills?

1042. To what degree will the team ensure that all members equitably share the work essential to the success of the team?

1043. To what degree are fresh input and perspectives systematically caught and added (for example, through information and analysis, new members, and senior sponsors)?

4.2 Variance Analysis: Data Center Networking

1044. Are there changes in the overhead pool and/or organization structures?

1045. Are control accounts opened and closed based on the start and completion of work contained therein?

1046. There are detailed schedules which support control account and work package start and completion dates/events?

1047. Are the overhead pools formally and adequately identified?

1048. How do you identify and isolate causes of favorable and unfavorable cost and schedule variances?

1049. What is your organizations rationale for sharing expenses and services between business segments?

1050. Did a new competitor enter the market?

1051. What are the actual costs to date?

1052. Is work properly classified as measured effort, LOE, or apportioned effort and appropriately separated?

1053. Budget versus actual. how does the monthly

budget compare to actual experience?

1054. Are procedures for variance analysis documented and consistently applied at the control account level and selected WBS and organizational levels at least monthly as a routine task?

1055. Are all elements of indirect expense identified to overhead cost budgets of Data Center Networking projections?

1056. How does the use of a single conversion element (rather than the traditional labor and overhead elements) affect standard costing?

1057. Is budgeted cost for work performed calculated in a manner consistent with the way work is planned?

1058. Is the market likely to continue to grow at this rate next year?

1059. Why do variances exist?

1060. Why are standard cost systems used?

1061. How do you verify authorization to proceed with all authorized work?

1062. What business event caused the fluctuation?

4.3 Earned Value Status: Data Center Networking

1063. If earned value management (EVM) is so good in determining the true status of a Data Center Networking project and Data Center Networking project its completion, why is it that hardly any one uses it in information systems related Data Center Networking projects?

1064. Verification is a process of ensuring that the developed system satisfies the stakeholders agreements and specifications; Are you building the product right? What do you verify?

1065. How does this compare with other Data Center Networking projects?

1066. Are you hitting your Data Center Networking projects targets?

1067. Validation is a process of ensuring that the developed system will actually achieve the stakeholders desired outcomes; Are you building the right product? What do you validate?

1068. How much is it going to cost by the finish?

1069. When is it going to finish?

1070. Earned value can be used in almost any Data Center Networking project situation and in almost any Data Center Networking project environment. it may be used on large Data Center Networking projects, medium sized Data Center Networking projects, tiny Data Center Networking projects (in cut-down form), complex and simple Data Center Networking projects and in any market sector. some people, of course, know all about earned value, they have used it for years - but perhaps not as effectively as they could have?

1071. Where is evidence-based earned value in your organization reported?

1072. What is the unit of forecast value?

1073. Where are your problem areas?

4.4 Risk Audit: Data Center Networking

1074. Does the team have the right mix of skills?

1075. Do you record and file all audits?

1076. Are audit program plans risk-adjusted?

1077. Have you reviewed your constitution within the last twelve months?

1078. Are procedures developed to respond to foreseeable emergencies and communicated to all involved?

1079. What are the risks that could stop you from achieving your KPIs?

1080. How do you govern assets?

1081. Does your auditor understand your business?

1082. What impact does experience with one client have on decisions made for other clients during the risk-assessment process?

1083. Is Data Center Networking project scope stable?

1084. Is the number of people on the Data Center Networking project team adequate to do the job?

1085. Are tools for analysis and design available?

1086. Do you have financial policies and procedures in place to guide officers of your organization/treasurer/general members?

1087. Is your organization an exempt employer for payroll tax purposes?

1088. Do you ensure the recommended rules of play and protocols are followed for your activity?

1089. Do requirements put excessive performance constraints on the product?

1090. What are the commonly used work arounds in high risk areas?

1091. Does your organization communicate regularly and effectively with its members?

1092. Are formal technical reviews part of this process?

4.5 Contractor Status Report: Data Center Networking

1093. Describe how often regular updates are made to the proposed solution. Are corresponding regular updates included in the standard maintenance plan?

1094. Who can list a Data Center Networking project as organization experience, your organization or a previous employee of your organization?

1095. If applicable; describe your standard schedule for new software version releases. Are new software version releases included in the standard maintenance plan?

1096. What process manages the contracts?

1097. How is risk transferred?

1098. What are the minimum and optimal bandwidth requirements for the proposed solution?

1099. What is the average response time for answering a support call?

1100. How long have you been using the services?

1101. Are there contractual transfer concerns?

1102. What was the overall budget or estimated cost?

1103. What was the final actual cost?

1104. What was the budget or estimated cost for your organizations services?

1105. What was the actual budget or estimated cost for your organizations services?

4.6 Formal Acceptance: Data Center Networking

1106. What is the Acceptance Management Process?

1107. How does your team plan to obtain formal acceptance on your Data Center Networking project?

1108. Was the Data Center Networking project work done on time, within budget, and according to specification?

1109. What can you do better next time?

1110. Who would use it?

1111. Does it do what client said it would?

1112. Who supplies data?

1113. Is formal acceptance of the Data Center Networking project product documented and distributed?

1114. Does it do what Data Center Networking project team said it would?

1115. How well did the team follow the methodology?

1116. Have all comments been addressed?

1117. Was the sponsor/customer satisfied?

1118. Was the Data Center Networking project goal achieved?

1119. What are the requirements against which to test, Who will execute?

1120. What was done right?

1121. Do you buy-in installation services?

1122. Was the Data Center Networking project managed well?

1123. Did the Data Center Networking project manager and team act in a professional and ethical manner?

1124. Did the Data Center Networking project achieve its MOV?

1125. Do you perform formal acceptance or burn-in tests?

5.0 Closing Process Group: Data Center Networking

1126. How well defined and documented were the Data Center Networking project management processes you chose to use?

1127. Who are the Data Center Networking project stakeholders?

1128. How dependent is the Data Center Networking project on other Data Center Networking projects or work efforts?

1129. Did you do what you said you were going to do?

1130. What areas does the group agree are the biggest success on the Data Center Networking project?

1131. What areas were overlooked on this Data Center Networking project?

1132. Were decisions made in a timely manner?

1133. What is the risk of failure to your organization?

1134. Were risks identified and mitigated?

1135. What level of risk does the proposed budget represent to the Data Center Networking project?

1136. What is the Data Center Networking project

name and date of completion?

1137. Is this a follow-on to a previous Data Center Networking project?

1138. What were things that you need to improve?

1139. Is the Data Center Networking project funded?

1140. Based on your Data Center Networking project communication management plan, what worked well?

1141. What can you do better next time, and what specific actions can you take to improve?

1142. Was the schedule met?

5.1 Procurement Audit: Data Center Networking

1143. Are periodic audits made of disbursement activities?

1144. Are fixed asset values recorded at historical cost?

1145. Are all complaints of late or incorrect payment sent to a person independent of the already stated having cash disbursement responsibilities?

1146. Is the procurement process well organized?

1147. Is it tested periodically, whether your organizations way of handling tasks is competitive in relation to price and quality?

1148. Are the journals and ledgers kept current for all funds?

1149. Where funding is being arranged by borrowings, do corresponding have the necessary approval and legal authority?

1150. Are risks in the external environment identified, for example: Budgetary constraints?

1151. Is it clear which procurement procedure your organization has opted for?

1152. Was the payment made to the supplier/

contractor within the time frames indicated in the contracts?

1153. Are trial balances taken weekly for general ledgers for all funds?

1154. Were no charges billed to interested economic operators or the parties to the system?

1155. Does the contract meet criteria of completeness and consistency?

1156. Does your organization maintain a current file of vendors and vendor catalogues?

1157. Were the specifications of the contract determined free from influence of particular interests of consultants, experts or other economic operators?

1158. Was suitability of candidates accurately assessed?

1159. Did the contracting authority offer unrestricted and full electronic access to the contract documents and any supplementary documents (specifying the internet address in the notice)?

1160. Proper and complete records of transactions and events are maintained?

1161. Was confidentiality ensured when necessary?

1162. Are unusual uses of organization funds investigated?

5.2 Contract Close-Out: Data Center Networking

1163. What happens to the recipient of services?

1164. Change in knowledge?

1165. Parties: Authorized?

1166. How is the contracting office notified of the automatic contract close-out?

1167. Parties: who is involved?

1168. Has each contract been audited to verify acceptance and delivery?

1169. Have all contracts been completed?

1170. How does it work?

1171. Why Outsource?

1172. How/when used ?

1173. Are the signers the authorized officials?

1174. What is capture management?

1175. Was the contract sufficiently clear so as not to result in numerous disputes and misunderstandings?

1176. Was the contract complete without requiring

numerous changes and revisions?

1177. Change in circumstances?

1178. Change in attitude or behavior?

1179. Have all acceptance criteria been met prior to final payment to contractors?

1180. Was the contract type appropriate?

1181. Have all contracts been closed?

1182. Have all contract records been included in the Data Center Networking project archives?

5.3 Project or Phase Close-Out: Data Center Networking

1183. Have business partners been involved extensively, and what data was required for them?

1184. Which changes might a stakeholder be required to make as a result of the Data Center Networking project?

1185. How often did each stakeholder need an update?

1186. Does the lesson describe a function that would be done differently the next time?

1187. Who exerted influence that has positively affected or negatively impacted the Data Center Networking project?

1188. What were the desired outcomes?

1189. Is the lesson significant, valid, and applicable?

1190. Is the lesson based on actual Data Center Networking project experience rather than on independent research?

1191. Is there a clear cause and effect between the activity and the lesson learned?

1192. Can the lesson learned be replicated?

1193. Does the lesson educate others to improve performance?

1194. What is a Risk Management Process?

1195. Was the user/client satisfied with the end product?

1196. Were messages directly related to the release strategy or phases of the Data Center Networking project?

1197. What could have been improved?

1198. What was the preferred delivery mechanism?

1199. How much influence did the stakeholder have over others?

1200. Who is responsible for award close-out?

1201. Who controlled the resources for the Data Center Networking project?

5.4 Lessons Learned: Data Center Networking

1202. What worked well or did not work well, either for this Data Center Networking project or for the Data Center Networking project team?

1203. Did the Data Center Networking project management methodology work?

1204. What did you put in place to ensure success?

1205. What were the major enablers to a quick response?

1206. How efficient were Data Center Networking project team meetings conducted?

1207. How timely was the training you received in preparation for the use of the product/service?

1208. What are the external dependencies?

1209. How clear were you on your role in the Data Center Networking project?

1210. What skills are required for the task?

1211. How much communication is socially oriented?

1212. Are you in full regulatory compliance?

1213. Were the Data Center Networking project

objectives met (if not, briefly account for what wasnt met)?

1214. How effective was the documentation that you received with the Data Center Networking project product/service?

1215. What rewards do the individuals seek?

1216. How much time is required for the task?

1217. What was helpful to know when planning the deployment?

1218. Why do you need to measure?

1219. How to write up the lesson identified – how will you document the results of your analysis corresponding that you have an li ready to take the next step in the ll process?

1220. Will the information remain current?

1221. Was the control overhead justified?

Index

management 1, 3-5, 9, 11-12, 19, 22-23, 36, 48, 60-61, 68, 71, 73, 80, 82-84, 87, 105, 114, 121, 133-138, 144-147, 150-151, 153, 157, 164, 166-167, 170, 172, 174, 178-180, 185-186, 190-192, 194-195, 199-200, 204-205, 208-210, 212-215, 221-222, 226, 228, 231, 235-236, 241, 247, 249-250, 253, 256-257

manager   7, 12, 25, 36, 41, 115, 127, 144, 187, 215, 248
Managers   2, 124
manages   79, 82, 127, 245
managing   2, 78, 124, 129, 131, 138, 222
Mandated   200-201
mandatory   218
manner   27, 90, 150, 204, 229, 240, 248-249
mantle 120
Mapping   61, 67, 72
market 26, 130, 159-160, 166, 239-240, 242
marketer   7
Marketing   117
markets   24
material   160, 187
materials   1, 144
matrices   142
Matrix 3-5, 130, 142, 186-187, 200
matter 39, 50
matters   221
maximizing   122
meaning   157, 227
meaningful   44, 109, 151, 238
measurable   33, 41
measure   2, 12, 27, 32, 36, 44, 46, 48, 50, 52-55, 64, 66, 75, 82-84, 90, 96-98, 103, 127, 132-133, 172, 176, 179-180, 182, 232, 258
measured   21, 47-50, 52-53, 55, 57, 76, 101-102, 181, 239
measures   45-48, 50, 56-57, 60, 62, 64, 67, 71, 86, 93, 98, 202, 216-217, 231
measuring   98
mechanical   1
mechanism   217, 256
mechanisms   133, 145
medium   242
meeting   39, 43, 95, 144, 154, 214, 227-228
meetings   30, 39-40, 213, 221, 257
megatrends   114
member   5-6, 32, 111, 120, 165, 200, 207, 214, 231, 237

preferred 256
pre-filled 9
prepare 166, 204, 207, 228
prepared 207
present 98, 110, 121, 130, 166, 231
presented 25, 226
presenting 224
preserve 40
preserved 62
pressing 126
pressures 160
prevalent 211
prevent 147, 179, 197, 209, 212, 223
prevented 223
preventive 202
prevents 19
previous 37, 159, 171, 245, 250
previously 130, 135, 194, 218
priced 151
prices 206
primary 45, 164
principles 232
printing 8
priorities 48, 56, 232
prioritize 180
priority 45, 51, 210
privacy 38
problem 17, 20, 22-25, 27, 29, 33, 37, 39, 47, 64, 130, 140, 167, 215, 221, 237, 242
problems 21-24, 26, 80, 86, 89, 100, 140-141, 145
procedure 167, 223, 228, 251
procedures 11, 78, 94-95, 97, 100, 136-137, 146-147, 153, 163, 173, 184, 204, 209, 216, 220, 228, 240, 243-244
proceed 240
proceeding 170, 191
process 1-7, 11, 31-32, 34, 37-38, 40, 42, 55, 60-65, 67-72, 76, 82, 92-93, 95-100, 125, 132-133, 135, 138, 141-142, 144-146, 163, 167, 184-185, 189-190, 194-195, 199-200, 208, 212, 220, 225-226, 229, 231, 235, 241, 243-245, 247, 249, 251, 256, 258
processes 48, 60-65, 67, 69-71, 73, 93, 97, 102, 125, 133, 146-147, 180, 185, 210, 212, 219, 222, 228, 249
procuring 212
produce 64, 125, 133, 163, 214

remaining 170, 176
remove 203
remunerate 83
rephrased 11
replace 44
replacing 138
replicated 255
Report 5-6, 79, 96, 190, 214, 225, 237, 245
reported 138, 145, 182, 209, 233, 242
reporting 60, 102, 120, 138, 145, 150, 216
reports 129, 190-191, 195
repository 137, 153, 208
represent 76, 218, 249
reproduced 1
reputation 114
request 5, 64, 216, 218-219
requested 1, 86, 216, 218
requests 216
require 41, 51, 65, 71, 93, 101, 127, 163, 194, 208
required 22, 24, 30, 32, 34, 41, 43, 58, 68, 73, 87-89, 93, 125, 140-141, 151, 156-157, 168, 190, 192, 197, 211, 213, 255, 257-258
requiring 129, 253
research 26, 111, 116, 198, 228, 255
resemble 206
reserved 1
reserves 209
reside 82, 208
resilient211
Resistance 211
resolution 70, 88, 145
resolve 17, 20, 24, 225, 227
resolved 174, 204
Resource 4, 117, 130, 136, 151, 163-164, 166, 190, 205, 214, 228
resources 2, 9, 18, 22, 25, 30, 40, 56, 59, 87, 93, 95, 100, 113, 117, 122, 125, 130, 136, 140, 151, 153-154, 157-158, 162, 164, 168, 173, 176, 178, 191, 208, 233, 238, 256
respect 1
respond 227, 243
responded 13
response 23, 26, 96-98, 100, 245, 257
responses 77, 222

urgent 216
usability   84
useful   78, 99, 148, 195
usefully 12, 25
usually 198
utility   169
utilized 150
utilizing 86
validate   55, 241
validated   31, 38, 40, 66, 137
Validation   241
valuable   7
values 121, 181, 189, 202, 251
variables   67, 96, 221
variance   6, 229-230, 239-240
-variance   172
variances   136, 150, 173, 205, 209, 239-240
variation   17, 31, 62, 95
variations   141
variety 90
vendor 76, 162, 191, 204, 252
vendors   19, 68, 87, 154, 252
verified 10, 31, 38, 40, 159, 166
verify   46, 48-51, 53-56, 58, 96, 98, 103, 133, 240-241, 253
verifying   47, 49, 52
version 245, 259
versions   37, 42
versus   227, 239
vested 105
viable   98, 149
vigorously   229
violate 146
violations   147
vision   121, 134
visions   132
voices   129
volatile 82
volume   186
Volumes   131
volunteers   228
warrant   225
warranty   1
weaknesses   130-131, 146, 160

CPSIA information can be obtained
at www.ICGtesting.com
Printed in the USA
BVHW041450230719
554170BV00012B/256/P

9 780655 820024